GCSE OCR 21st Century
Additional Science
Higher Workbook

This book is for anyone doing **GCSE OCR 21st Century Additional Science** at higher level.

It's full of **tricky questions**... each one designed to make you **sweat** — because that's the only way you'll get any **better**.

There are questions to see **what facts** you know. There are questions to see how well you can **apply those facts**. And there are questions to see what you know about **how science works**.

It's also got some daft bits in to try and make the whole experience at least vaguely entertaining for you.

What CGP is all about

Our sole aim here at CGP is to produce the highest quality books — carefully written, immaculately presented and dangerously close to being funny.

Then we work our socks off to get them out to you — at the cheapest possible prices.

Contents

Module B4 — Homeostasis

The Basics of Homeostasis 1
Negative Feedback 2
Diffusion 3
Osmosis and Active Transport 4
Enzymes 6
Controlling Body Temperature 8
Controlling Water Content 10
Treating Kidney Failure 13

Module C4 — Chemical Patterns

Atoms 15
Balancing Equations 16
Line Spectrums 18
The Periodic Table 19
Electron Shells 21
Group 1 — The Alkali Metals 22
Group 7 — Halogens 23
Laboratory Safety 25
Ionic Bonding 26
Ions and Formulas 27

Module P4 — Explaining Motion

Speed 28
Speed and Velocity 29
Velocity 31
Forces and Friction 32
Forces and Motion 33
Work 36
Kinetic Energy 37
Gravitational Potential Energy 38
Bungee Jumping 40

Module B5 — Growth and Development

DNA — Making Proteins 42
Cell Division — Mitosis 43
Cell Division — Meiosis 44
Development from a Single Cell 45
Growth in Plants 47
Stem Cells and Parkinson's 50

Module C5 — Chemicals of the Natural Environment

Chemicals in the Atmosphere 52
Covalent Bonding 53
Chemicals in the Hydrosphere 55
Chemicals in the Lithosphere 56
Chemicals in the Biosphere 58
Metals from Minerals 59
Electrolysis 60
Metals 62
Environmental Impact 64

Module P5 — Electric Circuits

Static Electricity 67
Electric Current 68
Circuits — The Basics 70
Resistance 71
Series Circuits 73
Parallel Circuits 74
Mains Electricity 75
Electrical Energy 78
The National Grid 80

Module B6 — Brain and Mind

The Nervous System 82
Reflexes 85
Learning and Modifying Reflexes 87
Brain Development and Learning 88
Learning Skills and Behaviour 89
Studying the Brain 90
Memory Mapping 91

Module C6 — Chemical Synthesis

Industrial Chemical Synthesis 93
Acids and Alkalis 94
Acids Reacting with Metals 96
Oxides, Hydroxides and Carbonates 97
Synthesising Compounds 99
Relative Formula Mass 102
Calculating Masses in Reactions 103
Isolating the Product and Measuring Yield 105
Titrations 106
Purity 107
Rates of Reaction 108
Collision Theory 110
Measuring Rates of Reaction 111

Module P6 — The Wave Model of Radiation

Waves — The Basics 112
Wave Properties 113
Wave Interference 116
Electromagnetic Radiation 118
Uses of EM Waves 119
Adding Information to Waves 121
Analogue and Digital Signals 122
Broadband and Wireless Internet 123

Published by Coordination Group Publications Ltd.

From original material by Richard Parsons.

Editors:
Amy Boutal, Ellen Bowness, Tim Burne, Tom Cain, Katherine Craig, Sarah Hilton, Kate Houghton, Sharon Keeley, Andy Park, Rose Parkin, Laurence Stamford, Jane Towle, Julie Wakeling, Sarah Williams.

Contributors:
Michael Aicken, Steve Coggins, Mike Dagless, Jane Davies, Mark A Edwards, Max Fishel, Paddy Gannon, Giles Greenway, Dr Iona M.J. Hamilton, Derek Harvey, Rebecca Harvey, Frederick Langridge, Barbara Mascetti, John Myers, Andy Rankin, Philip Rushworth, Adrian Schmit, Sidney Stringer Community School, Claire Stebbing, Pat Szczesniak, Paul Warren, Chris Workman, Dee Wyatt.

ISBN: 978 1 84762 001 9

With thanks to Jeremy Cooper, Ian Francis, Sue Hocking and Glenn Rogers for the proofreading.

With thanks to Laura Phillips for the copyright research.

With thanks to Waste Watch, www.wastewatch.org.uk, an environmental organisation working to change how we use the world's natural resources, for the information on page 65.

With thanks to The National Trust for the information on page 80.

Data used to construct pie chart on page 93 from "Concise Dictionary of Chemistry" edited by Daintith, J (1986). By permission of Oxford University Press. www.oup.com

Groovy website: www.cgpbooks.co.uk

Printed by Elanders Hindson Ltd, Newcastle upon Tyne.
Jolly bits of clipart from CorelDRAW®

Psst... photocopying this workbook isn't allowed, even if you've got a CLA licence. Luckily, it's dead cheap, easy and quick to order more copies from CGP – just call us on 0870 750 1242. Phew!

Text, design, layout and original illustrations © Coordination Group Publications Ltd. 2007
All rights reserved.

The Basics of Homeostasis

Q1 **Homeostasis** is an important process in the human body.

a) Define **homeostasis**.

....

....

b) Give **two** examples of conditions in the body that are controlled by homeostasis.

1. ....

2. ....

Q2 **Exercise** and **climate** can both have effects on the body.

a) Circle the correct words in the table to show the effects that **exercise** has on conditions in the body.

Temperature	increases / decreases
Water content	increases / decreases
Salt level	increases / decreases

b) What is the main risk to the body in a very **cold** climate?

....

Q3 Many **leisure activities** cause changes in the body.

Explain how each of the following can affect **blood oxygen levels**.
In your answer, name a condition that can occur during each activity.

a) Scuba-diving

....

....

b) Mountain climbing at high altitudes

....

....

....

Top Tips: Some animals don't have such a fancy homeostatic system to control temperature. Some reptiles have to bask in sunlight until their blood has warmed up before they can go about their business. I wouldn't mind lounging around in the sun for a couple of hours before work every day...

Negative Feedback

Q1 Write a definition of the term '**negative feedback**'.

....

....

Q2 The graph below shows how **negative feedback** systems operate in the body.

a) Circle the correct word in each pair to complete the sentence below.

In a negative feedback system the response produced has the opposite / same effect to the change detected — it increases / reverses the change.

b) Fill in the missing words in the labels on the graph.

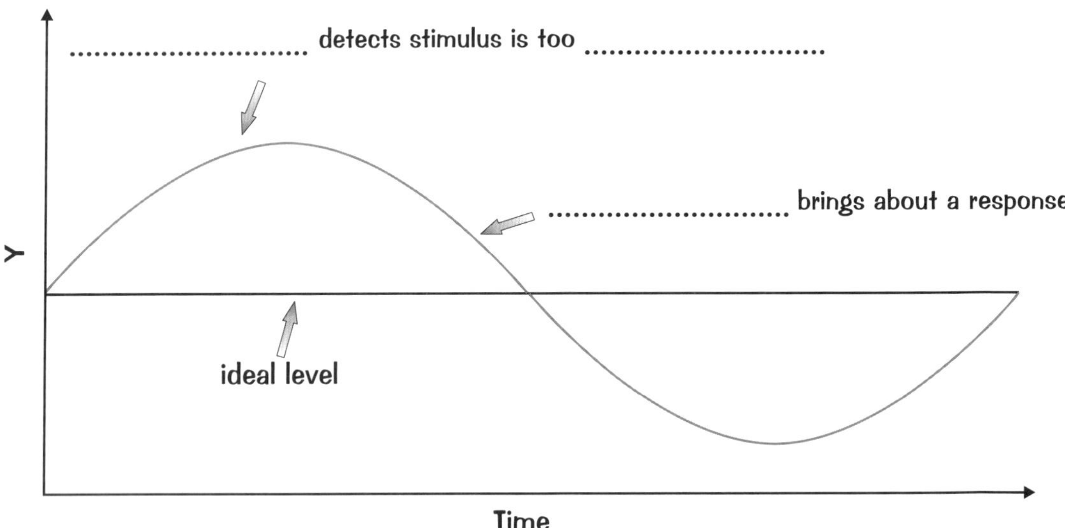

c) What name is given to the part of a negative feedback system that receives information and coordinates a response?

....

Q3 Some systems in **baby incubators** mimic natural negative feedback processes.

a) In what situation are baby incubators used?

....

b) Name a part of the incubator has the same role as the **receptor** in natural negative feedback systems.

....

Q4 What is the advantage of having **antagonistic effectors** in negative feedback systems?

....

....

Diffusion

Q1 Complete the passage below by circling the correct word in each pair.

> Diffusion is the direct / random movement of particles from an area where they are at a higher / lower concentration to an area where they are at a higher / lower concentration. The rate of diffusion is faster when the difference in concentration is bigger / smaller.

Q2 The diagram below shows some **body cells**. A **blood vessel** lies close to the cells.

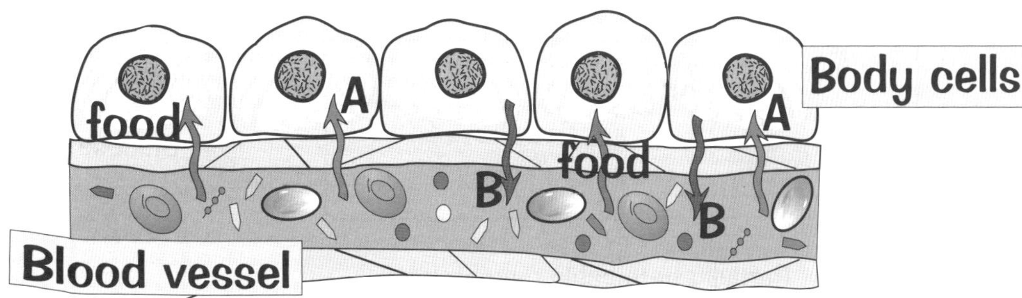

a) Is the concentration of food higher in the **blood** or inside the **cells**?

....

b) What gases are represented by each of the following:

i) The arrows labelled A ....

ii) The arrows labelled B ....

Q3 Tick the boxes to show whether the following statements are **true** or **false**.

		True	False
a)	Diffusion happens in gases, liquids and solids.	☐	☐
b)	Food moves from the body cells to the blood by diffusion.	☐	☐
c)	Diffusion can't happen across cell membranes.	☐	☐
d)	Oxygen diffuses from the blood into the body cells.	☐	☐

diffusion is an essential life process

Osmosis and Active Transport

Q1 Fill in the missing words to complete the paragraph.

> Osmosis is the overall movement of .... molecules across a .... permeable .... The molecules move from a region of .... water concentration to a region of .... water concentration. Osmosis is a special type of ....

Q2 Look at the diagram and answer the questions below.

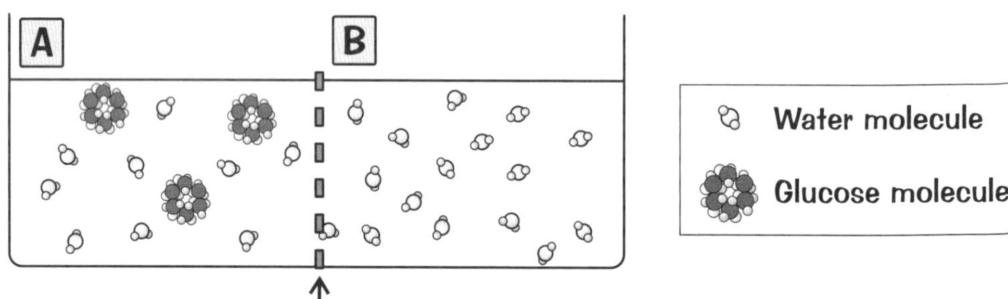

a) On which side of the membrane is there the **highest** concentration of water molecules?

....

b) Predict whether the level of liquid on side **B** will **rise** or **fall**. Explain your answer.

The liquid level on side B will ...., because ....

....

c) What is a partially permeable membrane?

....

....

....

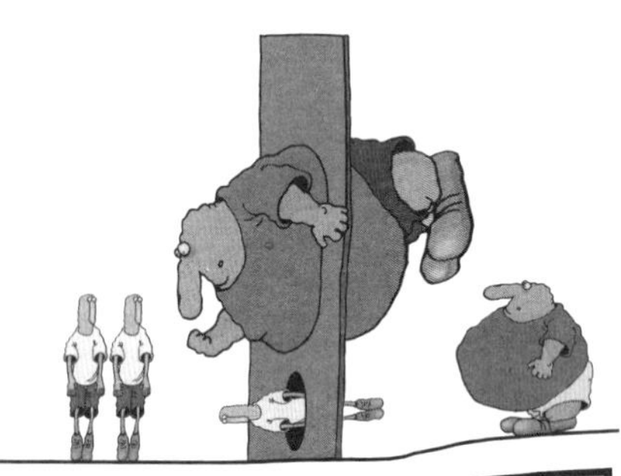

Top Tips: Osmosis, active transport and diffusion are some of the ways that things can move in and out of your cells. Osmosis and diffusion just simply happen without any help, whereas active transport needs a helping hand — it needs energy to get stuff moving.

Osmosis and Active Transport

Q3 **Active transport** is another important process within the body.

a) Define active transport.

....

....

b) Explain how active transport is different from diffusion.

....

....

Q4 Joan was making a **fruit salad**. She cut some oranges and grapes, sprinkled **sugar** over them and left them overnight. When she examined the fruit next morning it was surrounded by a **liquid**.

a) Suggest what the liquid might be. ....

b) Explain where the liquid has come from.

....

....

Q5 A **red blood cell** is in some very **dilute** blood plasma.

Plasma is the 'liquid' part of the blood.

a) Will water move **into** or **out of** the cell? Explain your answer.

....

....

b) Describe what will eventually happen to the cell.

....

Learning by osmosis

c) Describe what happens to an animal cell if it **loses** too much water.

....

d) Name the process by which some molecules are **moved** out of or into a cell against a concentration gradient.

....

Enzymes

Q1 a) Write a definition of the word '**enzyme**'.

....

b) What is the name of the area of an enzyme where the substrate joins and the reaction occurs?

....

c) In the box below, draw a sketch to show how an enzyme's **shape** allows it to break substances down.

Q2 This graph shows the results from an investigation into the effect of **temperature** on the rate of an **enzyme**-catalysed reaction.

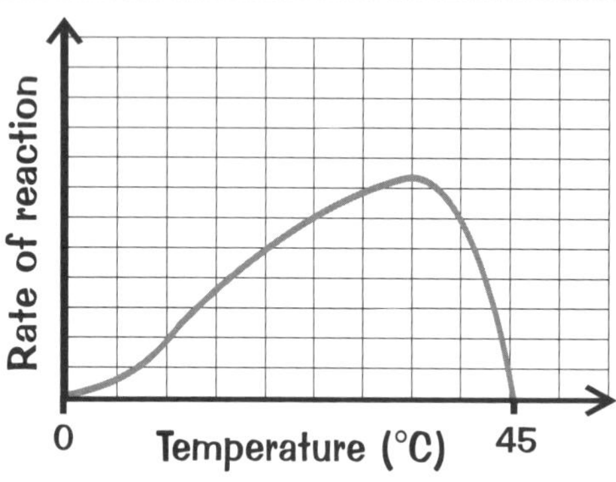

a) What is the **optimum** temperature for this enzyme?

....

b) Explain why at low temperatures a small increase in temperature increases the rate of the reaction.

....

....

c) What happens to the enzymes at **45 °C**?

....

Enzymes

Q3 Stuart has a sample of an enzyme and he is trying to find out what its **optimum pH** is. Stuart tests the enzyme by **timing** how long it takes to break down a substance at different pH levels. The results of Stuart's experiment are shown below.

pH	time taken for reaction in seconds
2	101
4	83
6	17
8	76
10	99
12	102

a) Draw a line graph of the results on the grid below.

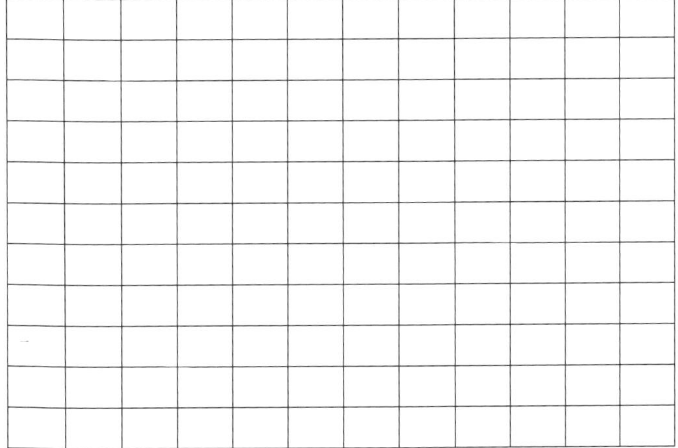

b) Roughly what is the **optimum** pH for the enzyme?

....

c) Explain why the reaction is very slow at certain pH levels.

....

d) Would you expect to find this enzyme in the **stomach**? Explain your answer.

....

Remember, it's very acidic in the stomach.

e) Describe two things that Stuart would need to do to make sure his experiment is a **fair test**.

1. ....

2. ....

Top Tips: Enzymes crop up all the time in Biology so it's worth spending plenty of time making sure you know all the basics. This stuff is also dead useful if you end up sitting next to someone with Desirability for a middle name at a dinner party — nobody can resist a bit of optimum pH chat.

Controlling Body Temperature

Q1 The human body is usually maintained at a temperature of about **37 °C**.

a) Which part of your **brain** monitors your body temperature to ensure that it is kept constant?

....

b) Name the location in the body of temperature receptors that monitor the **external** temperature.

....

c) What is the name of the **process** that enables the body to keep its temperature constant?

....

'Homeostasis' isn't the answer to this one.

Q2 The body has a number of **mechanisms** to control its temperature.

a) Which of these diagrams illustrates the skin's response to **hot** temperatures? Give a reason for your answer.

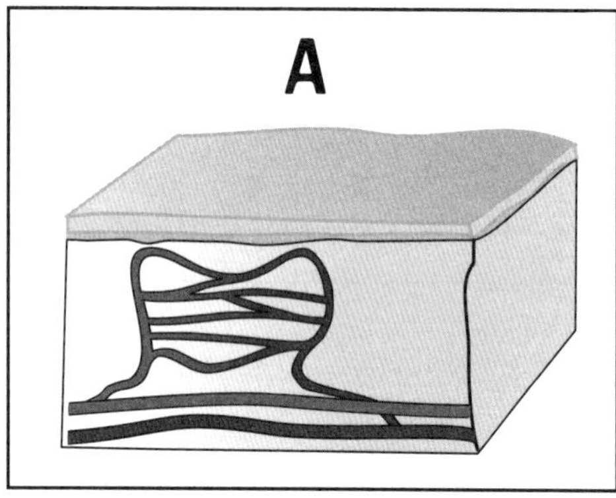

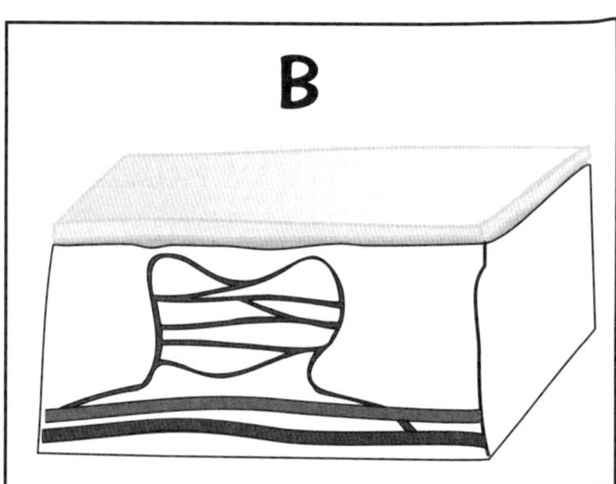

Diagram .... because ....

....

b) What other process can help the body to **cool down** when it's too hot?

....

c) Shivering can help the body to **warm up** when it's too cold.

i) Which parts of the body are the **effectors** in shivering?

....

ii) Explain how shivering helps to increase body temperature.

....

....

Controlling Body Temperature

Q3 A holiday maker with severe **heat stroke** is admitted to a hospital in Mexico.

a) List three possible **causes** of the patient's heat stroke.

1. ....

2. ....

3. ....

In Mexico, really hot Chilli can be a cause of heat stroke.

b) Circle the **symptoms** below that you might expect the patient to exhibit.

dizziness headache diarrhoea confusion muscle pain increased urine output

c) What happens to the normal mechanisms for controlling body temperature when you get too hot?

....

d) Describe how you would expect the patient to be **treated** when they first arrive at the hospital.

....

....

....

Q4 A group of **walkers** are found by a mountain rescue team after being missing in **poor weather** conditions on Mount Snowdon for **14 hours**. The mountain rescue team begin to assess the condition of the walkers. One of the walkers has a core body temperature of 34 °C.

a) Name the condition that the walker is suffering from.

....

b) Describe the **symptoms** the walker might exhibit.

....

....

c) Tick the correct boxes to show which of these **treatments** the patient should be given.

- [ ] Warm, dry clothing
- [ ] Placed into a bath of very hot water
- [ ] Warmed by a gentle heat source
- [ ] Exposed to very high temperatures, e.g. sitting in front of a roaring fire
- [ ] Have their hands and feet vigorously rubbed to warm up the extremities

Controlling Water Content

Q1 My brother was getting on my nerves, so I put him on a treadmill and turned the setting to high (just to keep him quiet for a bit).

Will my brother lose **more** or **less** water from the following body parts than he would if he sat still? Explain your answers.

a) Skin ....

....

b) Lungs ....

....

c) Kidneys ....

....

Q2 Mrs Finnegan had the **concentration of ions** in her **urine** measured on two days.

Date	6th December	20th July
Average air temperature (°C)	8	24
Ion concentration in urine (mg/cm^3)	1.5	2.1

Assuming Mrs Finnegan consumes the same amount of food and drinks and does the same amount of exercise every day, suggest a reason for the different ion concentrations in her urine.

....

....

Q3 The body needs to balance its water input and output.

a) Why is it important to maintain a balanced water level?

....

b) Name three ways that water is **gained** by the body.

1. .... 2. .... 3. ....

c) Name two **drugs** that can interfere with your body's water level.

1. .... 2. ....

Controlling Water Content

Q4 The **concentration** of urine and **amount** of urine produced are affected by many factors.

a) List three things that affect the **amount** and **concentration** of urine.

1. ....

2. ....

3. ....

b) Complete the following sentences by circling the correct word(s).

i) When you drink too little you will produce **concentrated** / **dilute** urine.

ii) On a hot day you will produce **more concentrated** / **less concentrated** urine than on a cold day.

iii) Drinking a lot of water will produce a **large** / **small** amount of urine.

iv) Drinking a lot of water will produce **dilute** / **concentrated** urine.

v) Exercising will produce **more concentrated** / **less concentrated** urine than resting will.

c) Why does **exercising** change the concentration of urine produced?

....

....

Q5 Some of the substances contained in the blood that enters the kidneys are listed below:

salt **water** **sugar** **urea** **blood cells**

a) List the things that are:

i) filtered out of the blood ....

ii) reabsorbed ....

iii) released in the urine ....

Billy the kid-ney bean

b) Is glucose reabsorbed back into the blood by diffusion or active transport?

....

c) Explain why the process you named in part **b)** is used.

....

....

Top Tips: Kidneys do loads of important jobs and that's why kidney failure is so dangerous. You can live with only one kidney though — so it's possible for some people with kidney failure to receive a donated kidney from a member of their family or from another suitable donor (see page 13).

Controlling Water Content

Q6 The concentration of water in the blood is adjusted by the **kidneys**. They ensure that the water content never gets **too high** or **too low**.

a) What is the name given to the kind of mechanism by which water content is regulated?

....

b) The hormone **ADH** is needed to control the body's water content. What do the letters ADH stand for?

....

The new kidney opera house was less popular than the old one.

c) Complete the diagram below by circling the correct word in each pair.

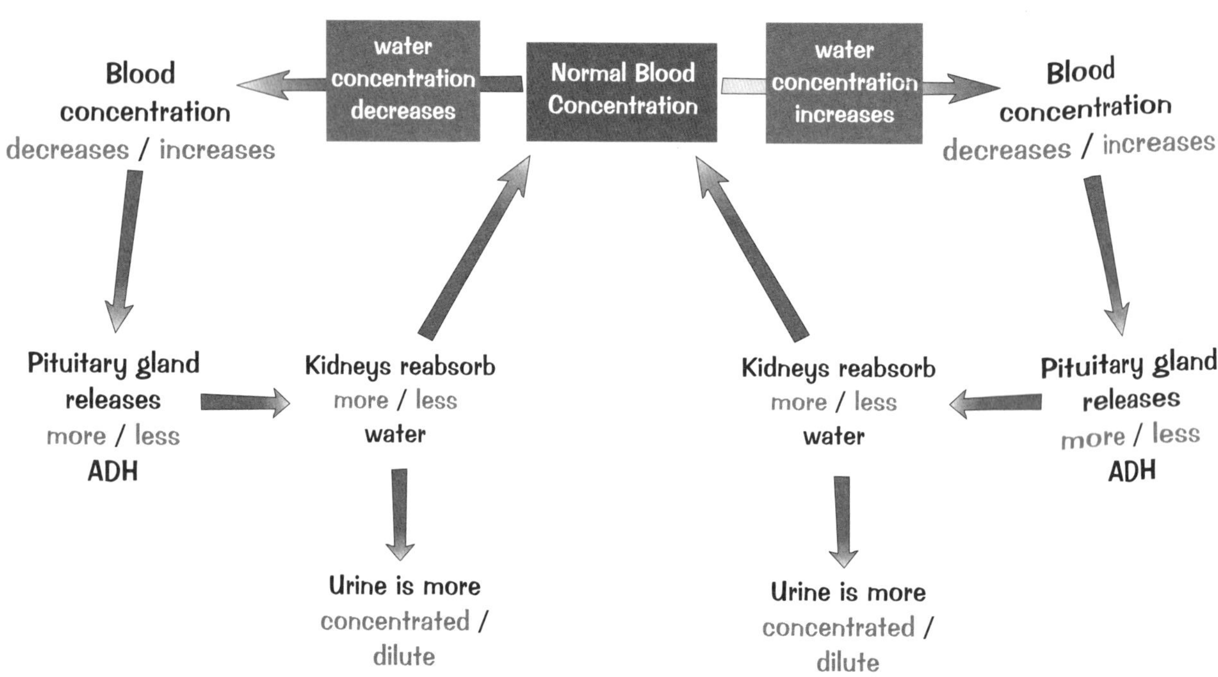

Q7 **Drugs** can affect the water content of the body.

a) Circle the correct word from each pair to complete the passage about the effect of **alcohol** on the water content of the body.

Alcohol **increases** / **decreases** the amount of ADH produced, causing the kidneys to reabsorb **more** / **less** water than they usually do. This **increases** / **decreases** the amount of water that leaves the body as **urine** / **sweat**, which can lead to **dehydration** / **overhydration**.

b) Explain how the drug **ecstasy** can affect the quantity and concentration of urine produced.

....

....

Treating Kidney Failure

Q1 Read the passage below and then answer the questions that follow.

Treating Kidney Failure

Around 40 000 people in the UK suffer from serious kidney failure. When the kidneys aren't working properly, waste substances build up in the blood. Without treatment kidney failure is eventually fatal.

Two key treatments are currently available for patients with kidney failure: dialysis — where machines do some of the jobs of the kidneys, or a kidney transplant.

Dialysis

Dialysis has to be performed regularly to keep the concentrations of dissolved substances in the blood at normal levels, and to remove waste substances.

In a dialysis machine (see diagram below) the person's blood flows alongside a partially permeable membrane, surrounded by a special dialysis fluid. The membrane is permeable to things like ions and waste substances, but not to big molecules like proteins — this mimics the membranes in a healthy kidney. The dialysis fluid has the same concentration of dissolved ions and glucose as healthy blood. This means that useful dissolved ions and glucose won't be lost from the blood during dialysis. Only waste substances (such as urea) and excess ions and water diffuse across the barrier.

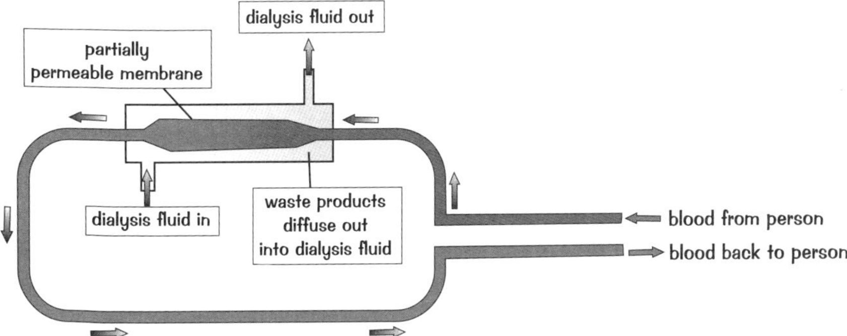

Patients with kidney failure generally need to have a dialysis session three times a week. Dialysis can be a very time-consuming process — each session can take over 3 hours.

Transplantation

Some patients are offered a kidney transplant. Healthy kidneys are usually transplanted from people who have died suddenly, and who are on the organ donor register or carry a donor card (provided their relatives give the go-ahead). Kidneys can also be transplanted from live donors — as we all have two of them and can live with just one.

Kidney transplantation has a high success rate but sometimes the donor kidney is rejected by the patient's immune system. The risk of rejection is minimised in the following ways:

- A donor with a tissue type that closely matches the patient is chosen.
- The patient's bone marrow is zapped with radiation to stop white blood cells being produced — so they won't attack the transplanted kidney. They also have to take drugs that suppress the immune system.

Treating Kidney Failure

a) A model of **dialysis** is shown below. No movement of substances has taken place yet.

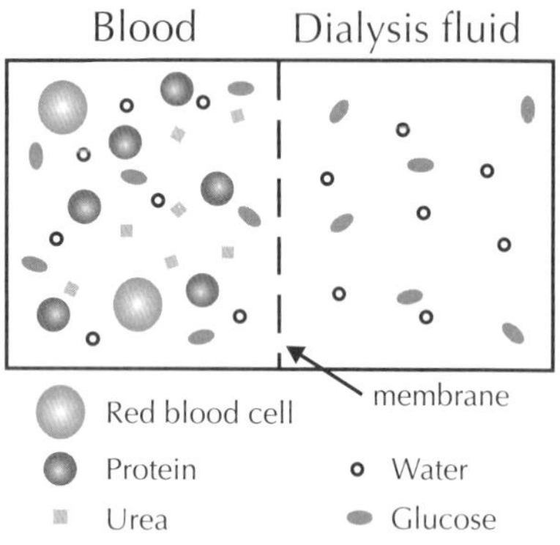

Blood | Dialysis fluid

membrane

Red blood cell
Protein
Urea
Water
Glucose

i) Which two particles will **not** diffuse across the membrane from the bloodstream into the dialysis fluid?

....

ii) Explain your answer.

....

....

iii) Which substance's concentration will **increase** in the dialysis fluid?

....

iv) What do you notice about the concentration of **glucose** on either side of the membrane? Suggest a reason for this.

....

....

b) The steps in dialysis are listed below. Number the steps in the correct order by writing 1 to 5 in the boxes.

- [ ] Excess water, ions and wastes are filtered out of the blood and pass into the dialysis fluid.
- [ ] The patient's blood flows into the dialysis machine and between partially permeable membranes.
- [ ] Blood is returned to the patient's body via a vein in their arm.
- [ ] Dialysis continues until nearly all the waste and excess substances are removed.
- [ ] A needle is inserted into a blood vessel in the patient's arm to remove blood.

c) i) Explain the advantage that a transplant has over dialysis for a patient with kidney failure.

....

ii) Give **two** precautions used to try and prevent a patient's body from rejecting a new kidney.

1. ....

2. ....

Atoms

Q1 Draw a diagram of a **helium atom** in the space provided and label each type of **particle** on your diagram.

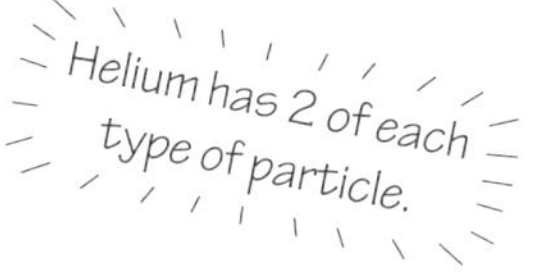

Q2 **Complete** this table.

Particle	Mass	Charge
Proton	1	
		0
Electron	0.0005	

Q3 **Complete** the following sentences.

a) Neutral atoms have a charge of ....

b) A charged atom is called an ....

c) A neutral atom has the same number of .... and ....

d) If an electron is added to a neutral atom, the atom becomes .... charged.

e) The number of .... in an atom tells you what element it is.

f) In a neutral atom, the number of protons is equal to the number of ....

Q4 Complete the table below to show the number of **protons** and **electrons** in atoms.

element	electrons	protons
magnesium	12	
carbon		6
oxygen		

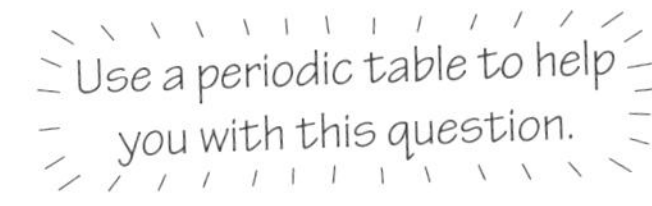

Use a periodic table to help you with this question.

Balancing Equations

Q1 Which of the following equations are **balanced** correctly? Tick the correct boxes.

		Correctly balanced	Incorrectly balanced
a)	$H_2 + Cl_2 \rightarrow 2HCl$	☐	☐
b)	$CuO + HCl \rightarrow CuCl_2 + H_2O$	☐	☐
c)	$N_2 + H_2 \rightarrow NH_3$	☐	☐
d)	$CuO + H_2 \rightarrow Cu + H_2O$	☐	☐
e)	$CaCO_3 \rightarrow CaO + CO_2$	☐	☐

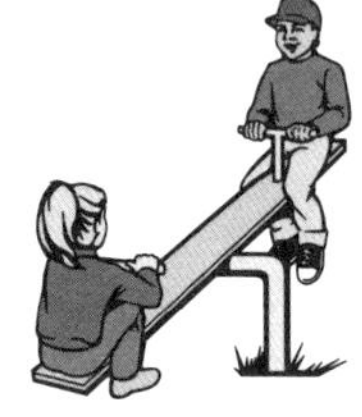

Alice and Bob were incorrectly balanced.

Q2 Here is the equation for the formation of **carbon monoxide** in a poorly ventilated gas fire. It is **not** balanced correctly.

$$C + O_2 \rightarrow CO$$

Circle the **correctly balanced** version of this equation.

$$C + O_2 \rightarrow CO_2$$

$$C + O_2 \rightarrow 2CO$$

$$2C + O_2 \rightarrow 2CO$$

Q3 **Sodium** (Na) reacts with **water** (H_2O) to produce **sodium hydroxide** (NaOH) and **hydrogen** (H_2).

a) What are the **reactants** and the **products** in this reaction?

Reactants: .... Products: ....

b) Write the **word equation** for this reaction.

....

c) Write the **balanced symbol equation** for the reaction.

....

d) What state symbol would be used in the equations above for:

i) water? .... **ii)** hydrogen gas? ....

Top Tips: The most important thing to remember with balancing equations is that you **can't** change the **little numbers** — if you do that then you'll change the substance into something completely different. Right, now that I've given you that little gem of knowledge, you can carry on with the rest. Just take your time and work through everything logically.

Balancing Equations

Q4 Write out the balanced **symbol** equations for the picture equations below (some of which are unbalanced).

a)  + →

....

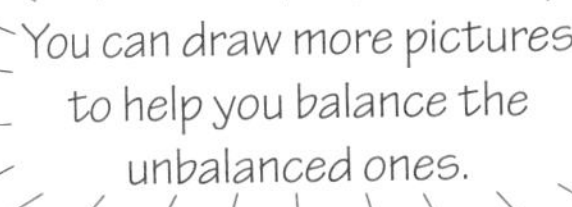

You can draw more pictures
to help you balance the
unbalanced ones.

b)  + →

....

c) 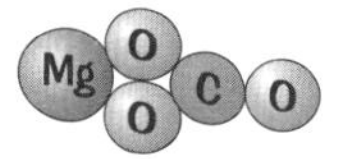 +  →  +  +

....

d) + 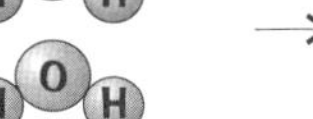 →  +

....

Q5 Add **one** number to each of these equations so that they are **correctly balanced**.

a) .... CuO + ... HBr → .... $CuBr_2$ + ... H_2O

b) .... H_2 + ... Br_2 → .... HBr

You need to have 2 bromines and 2 hydrogens on the left-hand side.

c) .... Mg + ... O_2 → $2MgO$

d) $2NaOH$ + ... H_2SO_4 → .... Na_2SO_4 + ... H_2O

Q6 **Balance** these equations by adding in numbers.

a) .... $NaOH$ + ... $AlBr_3$ → .... $NaBr$ + ... $Al(OH)_3$

b) .... $FeCl_2$ + ... Cl_2 → .... $FeCl_3$

c) .... N_2 + ... H_2 → .... NH_3

d) .... Fe + ... O_2 → .... Fe_2O_3

e) .... NH_3 + ... O_2 → .... NO + ... H_2O

Line Spectrums

Q1 A scientist is carrying out a **flame test** to identify the **metals** in three different compounds.

a) Complete the following sentence about flame testing.

> Some elements give a distinctive ....
>
> when placed in a ....

b) Draw lines to match the flame colours the scientist sees to the metal that is present.

lithium	yellow/orange
sodium	red
potassium	lilac

You have one hour to complete the test starting now.
FLAME
TEST
1 HOUR

Q2 a) Use the words in the box to complete the passage about **line spectrums**. Some words may be used more than once.

> light element line elements excited electron electrons

When heated, the .... in an atom become .... and release energy as .... The wavelengths of .... emitted can be recorded as a .... spectrum. Different .... emit different wavelengths of .... due to their different .... arrangements. This means that each .... will produce a different .... spectrum, allowing them to be identified.

b) As well as to help identify compounds, what else have line spectrums been used for?

....

Top Tips: I don't know why atoms get so excited at the prospect of being stuck in a hot flame — it certainly doesn't appeal to me. There's no accounting for some tastes... Anyway, line spectrums aren't as tricky as they might seem at first. Stick at it — they could easily come up in the exam — and you'll be passing with, errr... flying colours...

The Periodic Table

Q1 Use a **periodic table** to help you answer the following questions.

a) Name one element in the same period as silicon. ....

b) Name one element in the same group as potassium. ....

c) Name one element that is a halogen. ....

d) Name one element that is an alkali metal. ....

Q2 **Complete** this table.

Name	Symbol	Relative atomic mass	Proton number
Iron	Fe	56	
	Pb	207	
Xenon			54
Copper			

Q3 Select from these **elements** to answer the following questions.

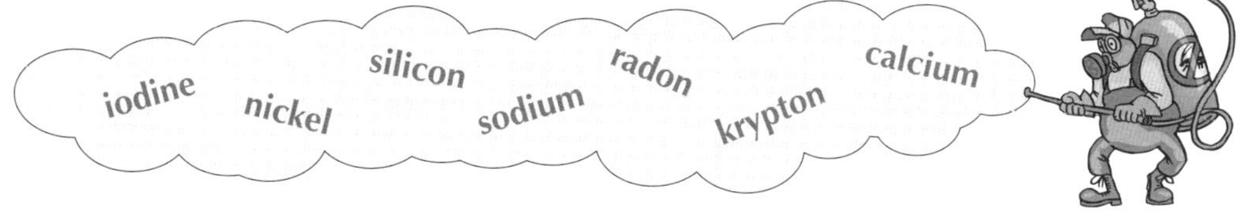

a) Which two elements are in the same group? .... and ....

b) Name two elements which are in Period 3. .... and ....

c) Name a transition metal. ....

d) Name a non-metal that is not in Group 0. ....

Q4 Choose from the words below to fill in the blanks in each sentence.

left-hand **right-hand** **horizontal** **similar** **different**
vertical **metals** **non-metals** **increasing** **decreasing**

a) A group in the periodic table is a .... line of elements.

b) Most of the elements in the periodic table are ....

c) Elements in the periodic table are arranged in order of .... proton number.

d) Non-metals are on the .... side of the periodic table.

e) Elements in the same group have .... properties.

The Periodic Table

Q5 Tick the correct boxes to show whether these statements are **true** or **false**.

		True	False
a)	The rows in the periodic table are also known as periods.	☐	☐
b)	Each **column** in the periodic table contains elements with similar properties.	☐	☐
c)	The periodic table is made up of all the known compounds.	☐	☐
d)	There are more than 70 known elements.	☐	☐
e)	Each new period in the periodic table represents another full shell of electrons.	☐	☐

Q6 Argon is an extremely **unreactive** gas. Use the periodic table to give the names of two more gases that you would expect to have similar properties to argon.

My property in the country.
Ar

1. ....

2. ....

Q7 Elements in the same group undergo **similar reactions**.

a) Tick the pairs of elements that would undergo similar reactions.

A potassium and rubidium ☐ **C** calcium and oxygen ☐

B helium and fluorine ☐ **D** nitrogen and arsenic ☐

b) Explain how the periodic table shows that fluorine and chlorine would undergo similar reactions.

....

....

Q8 Lithium is **less reactive** than sodium, which is **less reactive** than potassium. Fluorine is **more reactive** than chlorine, which is **more reactive** than bromine. Use this information to choose the correct words in the sentences below.

a) Reactivity **increases** / **decreases** as you go down Group I.

b) Reactivity **increases** / **decreases** as you go down Group VII.

Have a look at the positions of the elements in the periodic table.

Top Tips: The periodic table does more than just tell you the names and symbols of all the elements. You can get some other pretty important information from it too. For starters, it's all arranged in a useful pattern which means that elements with similar properties form columns.

Electron Shells

Q1 a) Tick the boxes to show whether each statement is **true** or **false**.

	True	False
i) Electrons occupy shells in atoms.	☐	☐
ii) The highest energy levels are always filled first.	☐	☐
iii) Elements in Group 0 have a full outer shell of electrons.	☐	☐
iv) Reactive elements have full outer shells.	☐	☐

b) Write out corrected versions of the **false** statements.

....

....

....

Q2 Describe **two** things that are wrong with this diagram.

1. ....

....

2. ....

....

Q3 Write out the **electron configurations** for the following elements.

Use a periodic table to help you with this question.

a) Beryllium ....

b) Oxygen ....

c) Silicon ....

d) Calcium ....

e) Aluminium ....

f) Argon ....

Q4 **Chlorine** has an atomic number of 17.

a) What is its electron configuration? ....

b) Draw the electrons on the shells in the diagram.

Cl

Group 1 — The Alkali Metals

Q1 **Sodium**, **potassium** and **lithium** are all alkali metals.

a) Highlight the location of the alkali metals on this periodic table.

b) Put sodium, potassium and lithium in order of increasing reactivity and state their symbols.

least reactive ....

....

most reactive ....

c) Describe the appearance of the alkali metals.

....

....

Q2 Circle the correct words to complete the passage below.

Sodium is a soft metal with **one** / **two** electron(s) in its outer shell. It reacts vigorously with water, producing **sodium dioxide** / **sodium hydroxide** and **hydrogen** / **oxygen** gas.

Q3 Archibald put a piece of **lithium** into a beaker of water.

Archibald

"squeaky pop!"

a) Explain why the lithium floated on top of the water.

....

b) After the reaction had finished, Archibald tested the water with universal indicator. What colour change would he see, and why?

....

....

c) Write a **balanced symbol equation** for the reaction.

....

d) i) Write a **word equation** for the reaction between sodium and water.

....

ii) Would you expect the reaction between sodium and water to be **more** or **less** vigorous than the reaction between lithium and water? Explain your answer.

....

Group 7 — Halogens

Q1 Highlight the location of the halogens on this periodic table.

Q2 Draw lines to match each halogen to its correct **symbol**, **description** and **reactivity**.

HALOGEN	SYMBOL	DESCRIPTION	REACTIVITY
bromine	Cl	green gas	most reactive
chlorine	I	grey solid	least reactive
fluorine	Br	red-brown liquid	quite reactive
iodine	F	yellow gas	very reactive

Q3 Decide whether the statements about the halogens below are **true** or **false**.

		True	False
a)	Chlorine gas is made up of molecules which each contain three chlorine atoms.	☐	☐
b)	The halogens can kill bacteria in water.	☐	☐
c)	The halogens become darker in colour as you move down the group.	☐	☐
d)	All the halogens have seven outer electrons.	☐	☐

Q4 Add the phrases to the table to show how the properties of the halogens change as you go **down** the group.

the melting points of the halogens

the reactivity of the halogens

the boiling points of the halogens

Increase(s) down the group	Decrease(s) down the group

Group 7 — Halogens

Q5 **Sodium** was reacted with **bromine vapour** using the equipment shown. White crystals of a new solid were formed during the reaction.

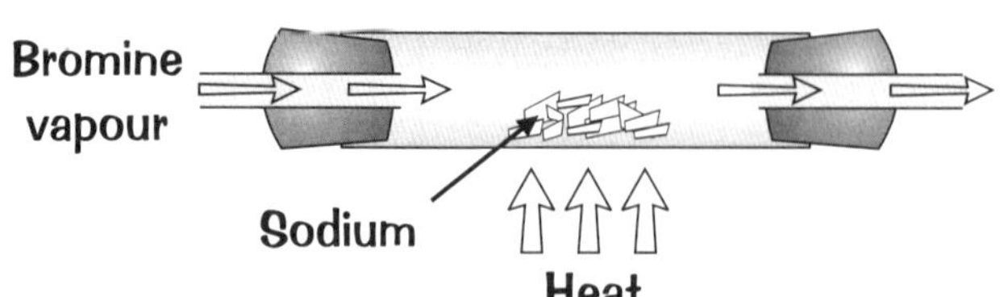

a) Name the white crystals.

....

b) Write a **balanced** symbol equation for the reaction.

....

c) Would you expect the above reaction to be **faster** or **slower** than a similar reaction between:

i) sodium and **iodine** vapour? Explain your answer.

....

ii) sodium and **chlorine** vapour? Explain your answer.

....

Q6 Equal volumes of **bromine water** were added to two test tubes, each containing a different **potassium halide solution**. The results are shown in the table.

SOLUTION	RESULT
potassium chloride	no colour change
potassium iodide	colour change

a) Explain these results.

....

....

....

b) Write a **balanced symbol equation** for the reaction in the potassium iodide solution.

....

c) Would you expect a reaction between:

i) bromine water and potassium astatide? ....

ii) bromine water and potassium fluoride? ....

Laboratory Safety

Q1 Fill in the meaning of each hazard symbol by choosing the correct label from the box.

corrosive	toxic	irritant
harmful	highly flammable	oxidising

a) ....

d) ....

b) ....

e) ....

c) ....

f) ....

Q2 The **alkali metals** are very reactive and so must be used with great care.

a) Explain why the alkali metals are stored under **oil**.

....

....

b) Suggest what should be done to any apparatus that is going to come into contact with an alkali metal.

....

c) Why must the solutions that the alkali metals form not touch the eyes or the skin?

....

Q3 The **halogens** must also be dealt with very carefully.

a) Why must the halogens only be used inside a fume cupboard?

....

b) Liquid bromine is **corrosive**. Explain what this means.

....

Top Tips: Laboratory safety isn't something that you can afford to skim over. It's important both for your exam and for when you're working in the lab. Unfortunately it's not enough to know that a symbol means that a chemical is dangerous — you need to know how it's dangerous.

Ionic Bonding

Q1 Fill in the gaps in the sentences below by choosing the correct words from the box.

protons	charged particles	repelled by	
electrons	ions	attracted to	neutral particles

a) In ionic bonding atoms lose or gain .... to form ....

b) Ions are ....

c) Ions with opposite charges are strongly .... each other.

Q2 Use this **diagram** to answer the following questions.

Na Cl + Na Cl −

a) How many electrons does **chlorine** need to gain to get a full outer shell of electrons? ....

b) What sort of charge does a **sodium ion** have? ....

c) What is the chemical formula of **sodium chloride**? ....

Q3 Tick the correct boxes to show whether the following statements are **true** or **false**.

		True	False
a)	Metals generally have fewer electrons in their outer shells than non-metals.	☐	☐
b)	Metals tend to form negatively charged ions.	☐	☐
c)	Elements in Group 7 gain electrons when they react.	☐	☐
d)	Atoms tend to form ions because they are more stable when they have full outer shells.	☐	☐
e)	Elements in Group 0 are very reactive.	☐	☐

Q4 Draw a 'dot and cross' diagram to show what happens to the outer shells of electrons when potassium and bromine react.

The diagrams in question 2 are 'dot and cross' diagrams.

Ions and Formulas

Q1 Here are some **elements** and the **ions** they form:

beryllium, Be^{2+} potassium, K^+ iodine, I^- sulfur, S^{2-}

Write down the formulas of four compounds that can be made using just these elements.

1. ....

2. ....

3. ....

4. ....

Make sure the charges on the ions balance.

Q2 Find the charge on the **chloride ion** in calcium chloride.

The formula is $CaCl_2$ and the charge on the calcium ion is 2+.

....

Q3 Use the table to find the **formulas** of the following compounds.

Positive Ions		Negative Ions	
Sodium	Na^+	Chloride	Cl^-
Potassium	K^+	Fluoride	F^-
Calcium	Ca^{2+}	Bromide	Br^-
Iron(II)	Fe^{2+}	Carbonate	CO_3^{2-}
Iron(III)	Fe^{3+}	Sulfate	SO_4^{2-}

a) potassium bromide ....

b) iron(II) chloride ....

c) calcium fluoride ....

Q4 **Aluminium** is in **Group 3** of the periodic table.
Complete the following sentences by choosing the correct word from each pair.

a) An atom of aluminium has **three** / **five** electrons in its outer shell.

b) It will form an ion by **gaining** / **losing** electrons.

c) The charge on an aluminium ion will be **3+** / **3–**.

d) The formula of the compound it makes with chloride ions (Cl^-) will be: $AlCl_3$ / Al_3Cl.

e) The formula of the compound it makes with oxide ions (O^{2-}) will be Al_2O_3 / Al_3O_2.

Speed

Q1 I rode my bike **1500 m** to the shops. It took me **5 minutes**.

Remember to convert the times given to the right units.

a) What was my average **speed** in **m/s**?

....

b) One part of the journey was downhill and I averaged 15 m/s over this 300 m stretch. How **long** did it take to cover this bit of the journey?

....

c) Going home I took a different route and my average speed was 4 m/s. It took me 8 minutes. How **far** is the journey home?

....

....

Q2 Paolo and some friends want to order a **takeaway**. Paolo writes down what they know about the two nearest takeaways:

Ludo's Pizza	*Moonlight Indian Takeaway*
• *Time taken to cook the food is 1/4 hour*	• *Time taken to cook the food is 1/2 hour*
• *Distance to the house is 6.5 km*	• *Distance to the house is 4 km*
• *Deliver on scooters with average speed of 30 km/h*	• *Delivery van has average speed of 40 km/h*

Remember to add on the time taken to cook the food.

Which takeaway should they order from to get their food the **quickest**?

....

Q3 **Speed cameras** can be used to catch speeding motorists. The section of road in the diagram below has a **speed limit** of **50 miles per hour**.

a) 1 mile = 1609 metres. Show that 50 miles per hour is about the same speed as 22 m/s.

....

b) The diagram below shows a car passing in front of a speed camera. The two pictures show the position of the car 0.2 s apart. The distance between each white line on the road is 2 m.

50

50

Was the car breaking the speed limit? Show your working.

....

Speed and Velocity

Q1 A **hare** challenges a **tortoise** to a **race**. The hare is so confident he'll win that he takes a nap on the way — he sleeps too long and the tortoise ends up winning. Here are some facts and figures about the race:

The **tortoise** ran at a constant speed of **5 m/s** throughout the race — pretty impressive.

The **hare** ran at **10 m/s** for **300 s** before falling asleep. He slept for **600 s** and then carried on at **10 m/s** towards the finish line.

The length of the **race track** was **5000 m**.

a) How far did the hare travel before falling asleep?

....

b) Add the information about the hare's run to the graph below.

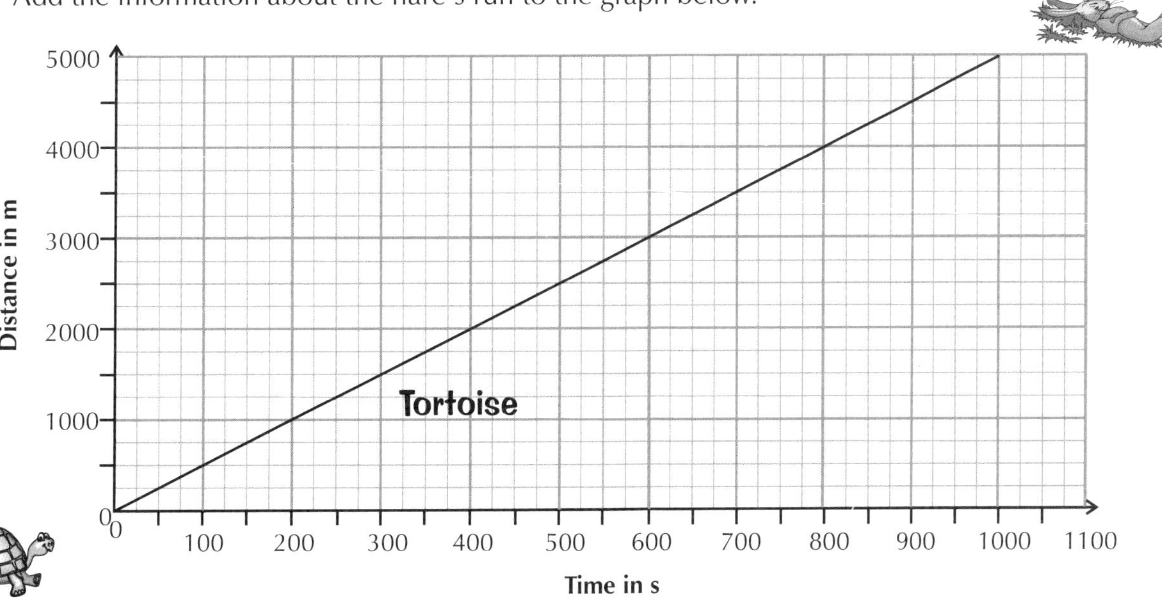

c) When did the tortoise overtake the hare?

....

d) How long did the tortoise have to wait at the finish line before the hare arrived?

....

Q2 The speed limit for cars on the **motorway** is **70 mph** (about 31 m/s). A motorist accelerated onto the motorway from a service station and was captured on a speed camera. He **denied speeding**.

Look at his **distance-time** graph.
Was the motorist telling the truth?

....

....

Think... you need to find the speed from a distance-time graph.

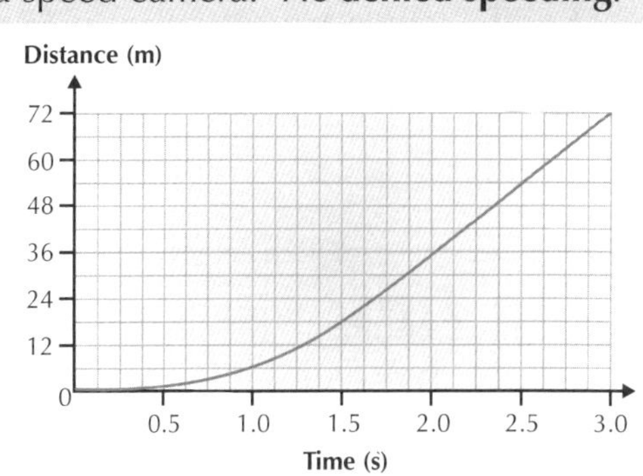

Speed and Velocity

Q3 The graph shows the motion of a **model train**.

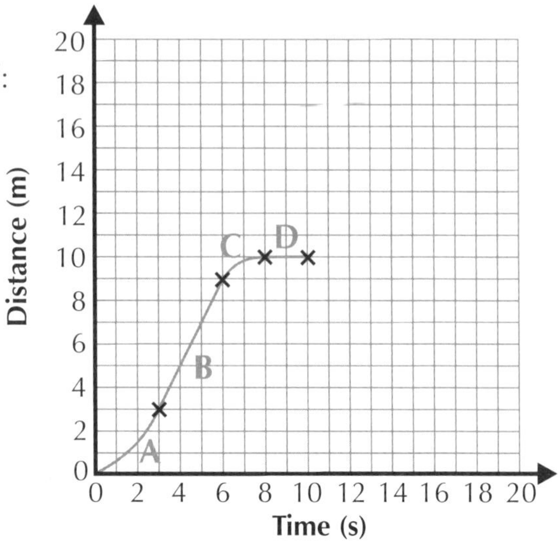

a) Describe the motion of the train in the sections marked:

A ....

B ....

C ....

D ....

b) What is the train's **average** speed in the first 8 seconds of the journey?

....

c) Calculate the **maximum** speed the train reaches.

....

d) Complete the graph by sketching to show the train:

i) accelerating to a higher speed than the maximum achieved before, then

ii) maintaining this speed for 2 seconds, then

iii) slowing to a stop.

Q4 A train travels 9 km from point **A** to point **B** in **10 minutes**.

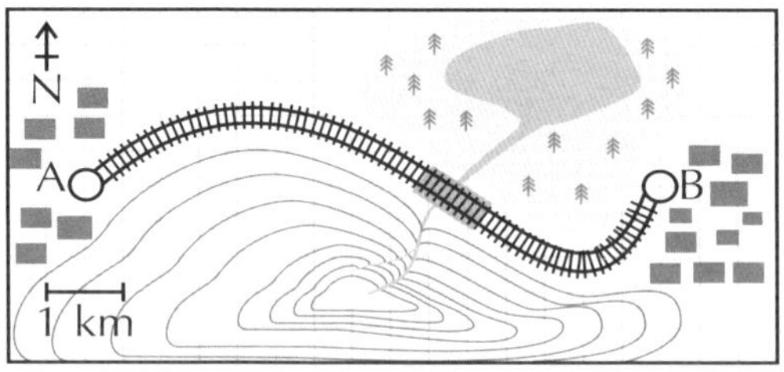

Tick the boxes to show whether the following statements are **true** or **false**.

		True	False
a)	The train's average velocity is 0.9 m/s due east.	☐	☐
b)	The train's average speed is 0.9 m/s.	☐	☐
c)	The train's average speed is 15 m/s.	☐	☐
d)	The train's average velocity is 90 m/s due east.	☐	☐

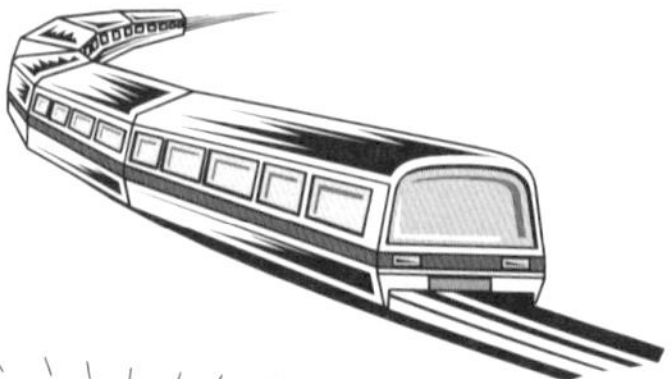

Top Tips: Remember, speed and velocity are basically the **same thing** (they're measured in the same way...), it's just that when you talk about velocity you've got to give a **direction**. As for all those distance-time graphs, they're not too hard once you've practised, so make sure you've got these ones right, and if you're still unsure, check up on all the facts and try again.

Velocity

Q1 Describe the **type of motion** happening at each of the labelled points on the velocity-time graph.

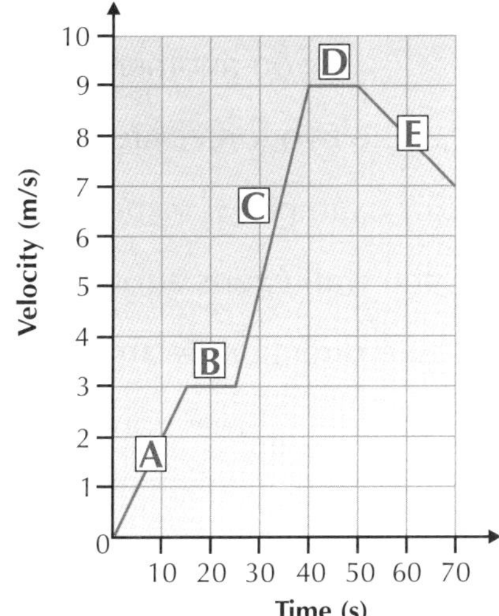

(A) ....

(B) ....

(C) ....

(D) ....

(E) ....

Q2 The **monorail** at Buffers' Theme Park takes people from the visitor centre to the main park and back again. It travels at the same **speed** on the outward and return journeys.

Buffers' Theme Park
Monorail
Visitor centre
Main park
River
Car park

The monorail's velocity on the outward journey is 12 m/s. What is its velocity on the return journey?

....

Q3 The distance-time graph and the velocity-time graph below both indicate the **same** three journeys.

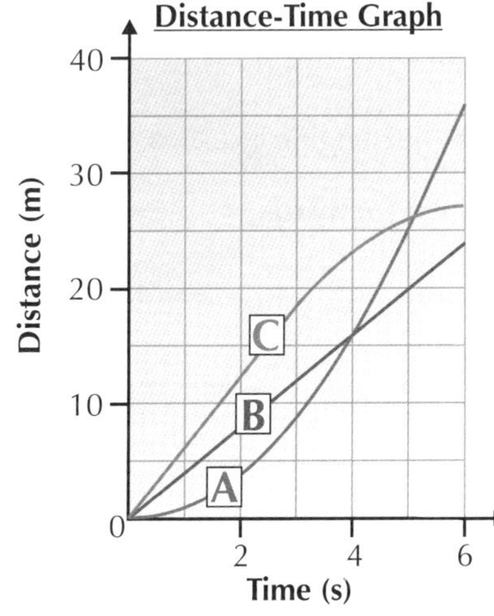

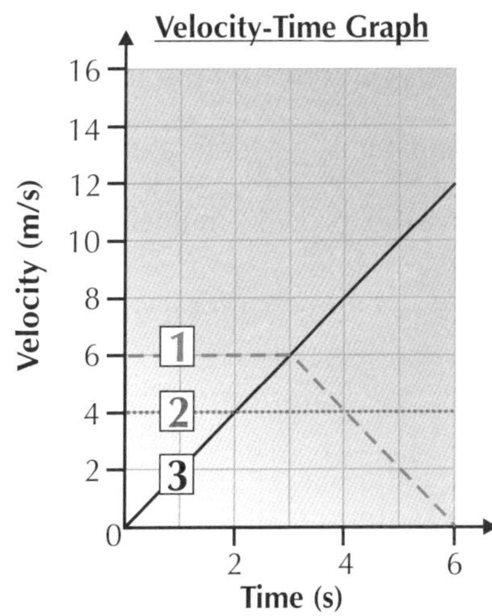

Draw lines to show how the distance-time and velocity-time graphs match up.

Line **A**	Line **1**
Line **B**	Line **2**
Line **C**	Line **3**

Forces and Friction

Q1 Complete the following passage.

When an object exerts a .... on another object, it experiences a force in return. The two forces are called an .... pair. For example, if someone leans on a wall with a force of 150 N, the wall exerts a force of .... N in the opposite direction — an '................................ and ....' reaction.

Q2 On the way down a slide, a penguin experiences friction.

a) Between which two objects is friction acting?

....

b) On the picture, label the **direction** in which friction is acting on the penguin.

c) Suggest how the penguin could **reduce** friction to speed up his slide.

....

Q3 A **jet engine** uses air to burn fuel, producing **exhaust** gases which accelerate backwards from the rear of the engine.

exhaust gases

a) Complete this sentence by circling the correct word(s).

The exhaust gases accelerate because the **air** / **jet engine** exerts **a force** / **friction** on them.

b) Explain how this process makes a jet aircraft move **forwards**.

....

....

Q4 A **flamingo** is standing on one leg.

a) Label the force A shown on the diagram.

b) Add a labelled arrow B to show the other force in the interaction pair.

c) Complete the following sentences about the two forces:

Force A is exerted by the .... on the .... Force B is exerted by the .... on the ....

Forces and Motion

Q1 A **teapot** sits on a table.

a) Explain why it **doesn't** sink into the table.

....

b) Jane picks up the teapot and hangs it from the ceiling by a rope.
What vertical forces now act on the teapot?

....

c) The rope breaks and the teapot accelerates towards the floor. Are the vertical forces balanced?

....

Q2 A **bear** rides a **bike** north at a constant speed.

a) Label the forces acting on the bear.

b) The bear brakes and slows down. Are the forces balanced **as** he slows down? If not, which direction is the resultant force in?

....

Q3 The diagram below shows the **forces** acting on an **aeroplane**.

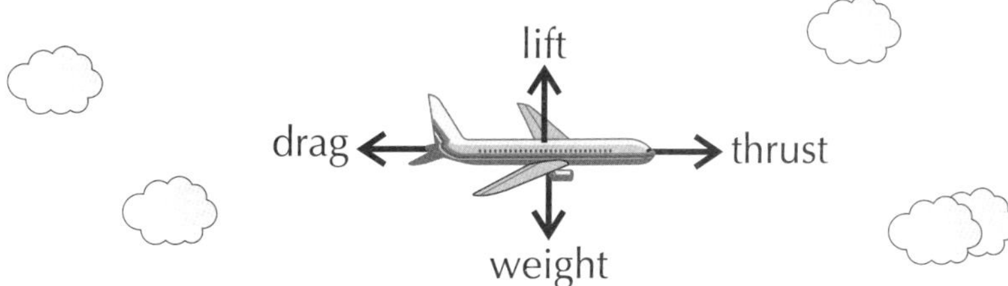

a) The aircraft is flying horizontally at a constant speed of 200 m/s. Which of the following statements about the aeroplane is true? Circle the appropriate letter.

- **A** The thrust is bigger than the drag and the lift is bigger than the weight.
- **B** The thrust is smaller than the drag and the lift is equal to the weight.
- **C** The thrust is equal to the drag and the lift is bigger than the weight.
- **D** The thrust is equal to the drag and the lift is equal to the weight.

b) What happens to the forces as the plane descends for landing and slows down to 100 m/s?
Choose the correct options to complete the following statements:

i) The thrust is **greater than / less than / equal to** the drag.

ii) The lift is **greater than / less than / equal to** the weight.

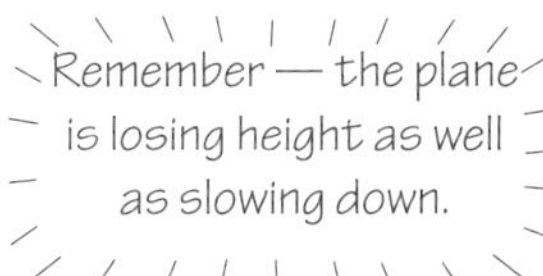

Remember — the plane
is losing height as well
as slowing down.

Forces and Motion

Q4 The **force diagram** on the right shows a **train** pulling out of a station.

1 500 000 N
6 000 000 N
1 500 000 N
1 500 000 N

Calculate the resultant force acting on the train in the following directions:

a) Vertical: ....

b) Horizontal: ....

Q5 Khaleeda helps Jenny investigate **falling objects**. Jenny lets go of a **tennis ball** and Khaleeda times how long it takes to fall. Khaleeda draws the distance-time graph — it looks like the one shown.

Distance from dropping point (m)
Time (s)
X
Y
Z

Which phrase below describes points X, Y and Z?
Explain your answer to each point.

forces in balance **reaction force from ground acts**

unbalanced force of gravity

X: ....

....

Y: ....

....

Z: ....

....

Q6 Place the following four **trucks** in order of **increasing momentum**.

Truck A	Truck B	Truck C	Truck D
speed = 30 m/s	speed = 10 m/s	speed = 20 m/s	speed = 15 m/s
mass = 3000 kg	mass = 4500 kg	mass = 4000 kg	mass = 3500 kg

....

....

(lowest momentum) .... , ... , ... , ... (highest momentum)

Top Tips: The main thing to remember about momentum (apart from the equation) is that it **changes** when a resultant force acts on an object. So if truck A started to brake, there'd be a resultant backwards force, and the truck's momentum would decrease. Makes perfect sense really.

Forces and Motion

Q7 A **boat** was travelling through the water in a straight line at constant speed. A wave hit the side of the boat, exerting a resultant force of **8000 N** for **1.2 seconds**.

a) Calculate the resulting change in the boat's momentum.

....

....

....

b) A few minutes later, the boat was hit by another wave. Its **change** in momentum was roughly **the same** as last time, but the force of the wave acted over a **shorter time**. What does this tell you about the average force acting on the boat during the second wave?

....

Q8 Modern cars are equipped with many **safety features** that reduce the **forces** acting on passengers during a collision.

a) Explain how a **seat belt** reduces the force acting on a passenger during a collision.

....

....

b) Give **two** other car safety features that work in a similar way.

....

Q9 A **1200 kg car** is travelling at **30 m/s** along the motorway. It crashes into the barrier of the central reservation and is stopped in a period of **1.2 seconds** (after which its momentum is **zero**).

a) Find the momentum of the car **before** the crash.

....

b) Find the size of the **average force** acting on the car as it stops.

....

....

c) Explain why the occupants of the car are likely to be less severely injured if they are wearing seatbelts made of slightly **stretchy** material.

....

....

Work

Q1 Circle one word in each sentence to make them correct.

a) Work involves the transfer of **force** / **heat** / **energy**.

b) To do work a **force** / **push** acts over a **distance** / **time**.

c) Work is measured in **watts** / **joules**.

Q2 Indicate whether the following statements are **true** or **false**.

	True	False
a) Work is done when a toy car is pushed along the ground.	☐	☐
b) No work is done if a force is applied to an object which does not move.	☐	☐
c) Gravity does work on an apple that is not moving.	☐	☐
d) Gravity does work on an apple that falls out of a tree.	☐	☐

Q3 An elephant exerts a constant force of **1200 N** to push a donkey along a track at a steady 1 m/s.

a) Calculate the work done by the elephant if the donkey moves **8 m**.

....

b) From where does the elephant get the energy to do this work? ....

c) Into what form(s) is this energy transferred when work is done on the donkey?

....

Q4 Ben's weight is 600 N. He climbs a ladder. The rungs of the ladder are 20 cm apart.

a) What force is Ben doing work **against** as he climbs?

....

b) How much work does Ben do when he climbs **10 rungs**?
(Ignore any 'wasted' energy.)

....

....

20 cm

c) How many rungs of the ladder must Ben climb before he has done **15 kJ** of work?
(Ignore any 'wasted' energy.)

....

....

Top Tips: Pretty much every 'work done' question you'll come across talks about moving something horizontally. Moving something vertically is exactly the same in principle though — you're just applying a force (at least equivalent to the object's weight) to move the object upwards.

Kinetic Energy

Q1 Find the **kinetic energy** of a 200 kg **tiger** running at a speed of 9 m/s.

....

....

Q2 A **golf ball** is hit and given 9 J of kinetic energy.
The ball's velocity is 20 m/s. What is its **mass**?

....

....

Q3 A 60 kg **skydiver** jumps out of an aeroplane and free-falls.
Find the skydiver's **speed** if she has 90 750 J of kinetic energy.

....

....

Q4 A large truck and a car both have a kinetic energy of **614 400 J**.
The mass of the truck is **12 288 kg** and the car **1200 kg**.

a) Calculate the **speed** of:

i) the car ....

ii) the truck ....

b) John is playing with his remote-controlled toy car and truck. The car's mass is 100 g. The truck's mass is 300 g. The car is moving twice as fast as the truck. Which has more kinetic energy — the car or the truck? Explain your answer.

....

Q5 Jack is riding his **bicycle** along a level road and has a total kinetic energy of **1440 J**. His dad gives him a push, exerting a force of **200 N** on the bicycle.

a) Explain why the push will **increase** Jack's velocity.

....

....

b) What assumption would you need to make to calculate Jack's increase in velocity? Why?

....

....

Gravitational Potential Energy

Q1 Fred works at a DIY shop. He has to load **28 flagstones** onto the delivery truck. Each flagstone weighs **250 N** and has to be lifted **1.2 m** onto the truck.

a) How much gravitational potential energy does **one** flagstone gain when lifted onto the truck?

1.2 m

....

b) What is the **total gravitational potential energy** gained by the flagstones after they are all loaded onto the truck?

....

c) How much **work** does Fred do loading the truck?

....

....

Q2 A **roller coaster** and its passengers are stationary at the top of a ride. At this point they have a gravitational potential energy of **300 kJ**. The full roller coaster has a mass of **750 kg**.

a) Draw lines to connect the correct energy statement with each stage of the roller coaster.

A B C D

A	minimum G.P.E., maximum K.E.
B	K.E. is being converted to G.P.E.
C	maximum G.P.E.
D	G.P.E. is being converted to K.E.

b) i) When the roller coaster is at half its original height, how much **kinetic energy** should it have?

....

ii) Calculate the speed of the roller coaster at this point.

....

....

iii) Explain why in real life the speed is **less** than this.

....

....

Gravitational Potential Energy

Q3 Jo is sitting at the top of a **helter-skelter ride** and her weight is **500 N**.

a) At the top of the helter-skelter, Jo's gravitational potential energy is **4000 J** greater than it was on the ground. How high up is she?

....

b) She comes down the helter-skelter and at the bottom her kinetic energy is **1500 J**. How much **energy** has been 'wasted' coming down the ride?

....

c) Which **force(s)** causes this energy to be wasted?

....

Q4 A skier with a weight of **700 N** rides a chairlift to a point **20 m** higher up a ski slope. She then skis back down to the **same height** as she got on the chairlift.

a) Calculate the **work done** by the chairlift in carrying the skier up the slope.

....

....

b) Assuming no energy is wasted, how much kinetic energy does the skier gain by skiing down the slope?

....

....

c) The skier has a mass of **70 kg**. What is the maximum **speed** she could reach as she skis down?

....

....

Q5 A toy cricket ball hit straight upwards has a gravitational potential energy of **121 J** at the **top** of its flight.

a) What is the ball's **kinetic energy** just before it hits the ground?

....

b) Calculate the **speed** of the ball at this time if its mass is **100 g**.

....

Top Tips: Kinetic energy, gravitational potential energy, work done... they're all measured in joules, so they're all energy. If you 'do work' on something, you're converting energy — by exerting a force on the object which makes it move. If you start an object moving or make it speed up you've given it some K.E. If you move the object away from the ground, you've given it some G.P.E.

Bungee Jumping

Q1 Read the passage below and answer the questions that follow.

Bungee jumping is a popular sport and recreational activity, carefully managed to minimise the risks. Millions of jumps have been successfully and safely completed around the world, with the highest commercial jump now standing at 233 m (764 ft) in Macau, China.

A bungee jumper at the Macau jump starts on the 233 m high platform, then gains speed for 5 seconds before the pull of the bungee cord begins to affect their freefall, as shown on the graph.

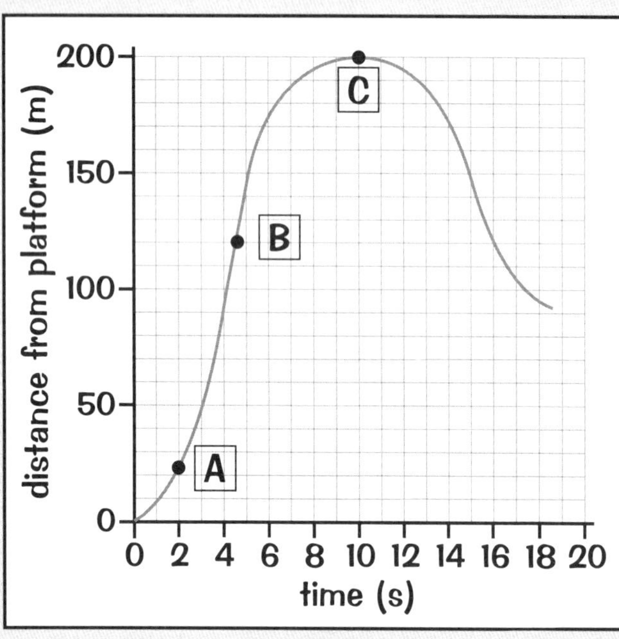

After 10 seconds they come to within 30 m or so of the ground before rebounding upwards. Jumpers can reach speeds of up to 200 km/h.

A common misconception about the dangers of bungee jumping is the idea that the cord may snap. Bungee cord is made from a tightly wound matrix of extremely strong elastic fibres, and most cords can hold up to 1000 kg before snapping.

The most common cause of bungee accidents is thought to be overestimation of the length of bungee cord needed. People expect the cord to slow the jumper down as soon as it reaches its natural length (the length of the cord when nothing is suspended from it), but this is not the case — at its natural length, the cord has virtually no resistance, and the jumper carries on gaining speed for some time before they are slowed down. The cords used at Macau have a natural length of 50 m.

a) Using the distance-time graph in the passage, describe the motion of the jumper at:

i) point A .... **ii)** point B ....

iii) point C ....

b) Describe the **vertical forces** acting on the jumper at **point C**.

....

....

c) How many times longer than its natural length is the bungee cord at **point C**?

....

Bungee Jumping

d) Using the graph, calculate the **average speed** (in m/s) of the jumper during their descent.

....

e) **i)** Determine the **maximum** speed the bungee jumper reaches in metres per second.

....

ii) Using the axes below, sketch a graph of the first **13 seconds** of the jump at Macau.

velocity (m/s): 60, 40, 20, 0, –20, –40

time (s): 1 2 3 4 5 6 7 8 9 10 11 12 13

iii) How long would it take to travel from the platform to the ground at the jumper's top speed?

....

iv) If the jumper's mass was **75 kg** , what would be his momentum at this speed?

....

f) After his jump, a jumper weighing **950 N** climbs back up to the start point, a vertical distance of **233 m**. Calculate the work he does during this climb.

....

g) A tourist at the Macau jump decides to climb up to the bungee platform to take some pictures. As he reaches the top, he drops his camera. The camera weighs **2 N** (mass = **0.2 kg**). Calculate its **speed** as it hits the ground below.

G.P.E. = K.E

....

....

....

h) Skydivers reach speeds similar to those of bungee jumpers. By streamlining their shape, they can reach around 90 m/s (about 200 mph). However, they struggle to go any faster than this, no matter how long they're falling for. Suggest why.

Think about the vertical forces acting on them at constant speed...

....

....

....

DNA — Making Proteins

Q1 The following questions are about **DNA**.

a) What is the **function** of DNA?

....

b) What name is given to the **shape** of a DNA molecule? ....

c) How many different bases make up the DNA structure? ....

d) Which bases pair up together?

....

Q2 Tick the boxes to show whether the following statements are **true** or **false**.

		True	False
a)	Genes are sections of DNA that code for specific proteins.	☐	☐
b)	Each amino acid is coded for by a set of four base pairs.	☐	☐
c)	Each cell contains different genes, which is why we have different types of cell.	☐	☐
d)	Proteins are made at ribosomes.	☐	☐
e)	RNA is a messenger molecule that communicates between DNA and the ribosomes.	☐	☐
f)	RNA contains two strands, like DNA.	☐	☐

Q3 On the section of **DNA** shown:

A G G C T A G C C A A T C G C C G A A G C T C A

T C C G A T C G G T T A G C G

a) Complete the lower sequence of bases.

b) Calculate how many **amino acids** this section of DNA codes for.

....

Q4 Answer the following questions to explain how a section of code on a **DNA molecule** can be used to build a new **protein**.

a) How is a molecule of **messenger RNA** formed from a molecule of DNA?

....

....

b) How do **RNA** and **ribosomes** work together to build proteins?

....

....

Cell Division — Mitosis

Q1 Decide whether the following statements are **true** or **false**.

		True	False
a)	As a cell grows the number of organelles increases.	☐	☐
b)	Chromosomes are found in the cytoplasm of a cell.	☐	☐
c)	Before a cell divides by mitosis, it duplicates its DNA.	☐	☐
d)	Mitosis is where a cell divides to create two genetically identical copies.	☐	☐
e)	Nucleotides are made up of chains of DNA.	☐	☐
f)	Organisms use mitosis in order to grow.	☐	☐
g)	Organisms do not use mitosis to replace damaged cells.	☐	☐

Q2 Complete the following passage using the words below.

nucleotides **chromosomes** **DNA strands** **bases** **cross-links**

Before a cell splits in two by mitosis, everything in the cell is copied. To copy ...., the molecule of DNA splits, then the bases on free-floating .... pair up with matching bases on the single strands of DNA. Once matched, ... form between the .... and the old ...., and the nucleotides on the new strand are joined together.

Q3 The following diagram shows the different stages of **mitosis**.
Write a short description to explain each stage.

a) ....

b) ....

c) ....

....

d) ....

....

e) ....

Cell Division — Meiosis

Q1 Tick the boxes below to show which statements are true of **mitosis, meiosis** or **both**.

		Mitosis	Meiosis
a)	Halves the number of chromosomes.	☐	☐
b)	Chromosomes line up in the centre of the cell.	☐	☐
c)	Forms cells that are genetically different.	☐	☐
d)	In humans, it only happens in the reproductive organs.	☐	☐

Q2 Draw lines to match the descriptions of the stage of **meiosis** to the right diagram below. The first one has been done for you.

a)

b)

c)

d)

e)

The pairs are pulled apart, mixing up the mother's and father's chromosomes into the new cells. This creates genetic variation.

Before the cell starts to divide it duplicates its DNA to produce an exact copy.

There are now four gametes, each containing half the original number of chromosomes.

For the first meiotic division the chromosomes line up in their pairs across the centre of the cell.

The chromosomes line up across the centre of the nucleus ready for the second division, and the left and right arms are pulled apart.

Q3 During sexual reproduction, two **gametes** combine to form a new individual.

a) What are gametes? ....

b) Explain why gametes have **half** the usual number of chromosomes.

....

....

Top Tips: I've tried for ages to come up with a good way of remembering which is mitosis and which is meiosis. Unfortunately I got stuck at "My toes(ies) grow(sies)...", which is rather lame if I may say so myself. I hope for your sake you come up with something better. Good luck...

Development from a Single Cell

Q1 The following terms are related to **stem cells**. Explain what each term means.

a) specialised cells ....

b) differentiation ....

c) undifferentiated cells ....

Q2 How are **embryonic** stem cells different from **adult** stem cells?

....

....

....

Q3 Describe a way that **stem cells** are currently used in **medicine**.

....

....

....

Raymond pondered how long his bone marrow would take to grow.

Q4 Some **stem cells** are extracted from a **cloned** embryo. Number the stages in the correct order to show how a cloned embryo is produced. The first one has been done for you.

- ...1... Take an egg cell.
- .... Grow the embryo.
- .... Insert a complete set of chromosomes from the adult you want to clone.
- .... Remove the genetic material.
- .... Stimulate the cell under the right conditions to reactivate certain genes.
- .... Extract embryonic stem cells.

Top Tips: Stem cells are cutting-edge stuff right now. You'll probably see loads more of them in the news in the future as scientists use them to try to find new cures for disorders like Parkinson's.

Development from a Single Cell

Q5 Circle the cell types below that are **specialised**.

differentiated cell gamete red blood cell

embryonic stem cell nerve cell

Q6 Tick the correct boxes to show whether the following statements are **true** or **false**.

		True	False
a)	Cells in an early embryo are unspecialised.	☐	☐
b)	Blood cells are undifferentiated.	☐	☐
c)	Nerve cells are specialised cells.	☐	☐
d)	Adult stem cells are as versatile as embryonic stem cells.	☐	☐
e)	Stem cells in bone marrow can differentiate into any type of cell.	☐	☐

Q7 In the future, **embryonic stem cells** might be used to replace faulty cells in sick people. Match the problems below to the potential cures which could be made with stem cells.

diabetes	**heart muscle cells**
paralysis	**insulin-producing cells**
heart disease	**brain cells**
Alzheimer's	**nerve cells**

Q8 Explain how scientists try to get cultures of one **specific** type of cell from **embryonic stem cells**.

....

....

....

Q9 What is the **advantage** of treating a disease using stem cells from **cloned** embryos that are genetically identical to the patient?

....

....

....

Growth in Plants

Q1 Give two differences in **growth** between plants and animals.

1. ....

2. ....

Q2 Decide whether the following statements are **true** or **false**.

		True	False
a)	Meristem tissue at the tips of stems contains the plant equivalent of adult stem cells.	☐	☐
b)	The cells in the meristem lose their properties as the plant ages.	☐	☐
c)	Meristem tissue is generated in the stem of the plant and transported to the roots and shoots where it is needed for growth.	☐	☐
d)	Cells produced by dividing meristem cells can differentiate to become cells in flowers.	☐	☐
e)	Differentiation is triggered by turning certain genes on or off.	☐	☐
f)	Cells behind the meristem tissue grow via cell elongation.	☐	☐

Q3 Three **plant shoots** were set up with a **light stimulus**. The diagram shows the shape of each shoot before and after.

a) Which part of the plant shoot is most sensitive to light?

....

b) Which plant **hormone** controls the growth of the tip?

....

c) On each picture, shade in the region that contains the **most** of this hormone.

Q4 **Phototropism** is necessary for the survival of plants.

a) Explain what **positive** and **negative** phototropism are.

....

....

b) Explain why phototropism is needed for a plant to survive.

....

....

Growth in Plants

Q5 Decide whether the following statements are **true** or **false**.

		True	False
a)	Plant shoots grow away from light.	☐	☐
b)	Plant roots grow towards light.	☐	☐
c)	Positive phototropism ensures that roots grow deep into the soil for nutrients.	☐	☐
d)	If the tip of a shoot is removed, the shoot may stop growing.	☐	☐

Q6 Sally takes **two cuttings** from her favourite plant and tries to **grow both** using rooting powder to produce new plants. One cutting grows **well** but the other **doesn't**. Which of the cuttings shown would you expect to **grow best**, and why?

cutting 1

cutting 2

....

....

....

Q7 Arnold placed some **seedlings** in a closed shoe box which had a small hole in the top to let light in. He left them in the box for **five days**. The change in the appearance of one of the seedlings is shown in the diagram below.

start — bean

5 days later — bean

a) Label the root and the shoot on each of the diagrams.

b) Where are the hormones that cause the root and shoot to grow differently produced?

....

c) Explain the results observed for the shoot and the root in terms of their response to **light**.

i) the shoot ....

....

ii) the root ....

....

Top Tips: You often hear about athletes being caught by random drugs tests for using hormones to beef themselves up a bit — I've never heard of any gardeners having their prize vegetable carted off for a random auxin testing though. Hmmmm...

Growth in Plants

Q8 Barry is investigating the effect of **auxin concentration** on the growth of the roots in some **identical plant cuttings**. His measurements are shown in the table.

a) What are plant cuttings? ....

The table shows the effect of auxin concentration on root growth over a week.

Concentration of auxin (parts per million)	0	0.001	0.01	0.1	1
Increase of root length (mm)	6	12	8	3	1

b) Plot a bar chart of the increase in root length against the concentration of auxin on the grid below.

c) What do the results suggest is the best concentration of auxin to use to encourage growth?

....

d) What do you notice about the effect of high auxin concentration on the rate of growth?

....

....

e) Give one thing that Barry should have done to make the test fair.

....

Q9 Two shoot tips were removed from young plants. Agar blocks **soaked in auxin** were placed on the **cut ends** of the **shoots** as shown in the diagram, and they were placed in the dark. The auxin **soaks** into the stem where the block touches it.

a) Describe the expected responses of shoots A and B to this treatment.

i) Shoot A ....

ii) Shoot B ....

b) Explain your answers.

i) Shoot A ....

....

ii) Shoot B ....

....

Stem Cells and Parkinson's

Q1 Read the passage about using **stem cells** to treat **Parkinson's**, then answer the questions that follow.

Stem cells have been one of the decade's hottest research topics, but have so far not lived up to their promise of being a wonder-cure. However, there have recently been promising results from studies using both adult and embryonic stem cells to treat Parkinson's disease.

Symptoms of Parkinson's disease include shaking movements, muscle stiffness and difficulty in moving. Parkinson's can also cause problems with handwriting, speech and balance, leaving many sufferers with a poor quality of life.

The symptoms of Parkinson's are caused by the death of nerve cells that produce a chemical called dopamine. Dopamine carries signals in the parts of the brain controlling movement — as the levels decline, sufferers' ability to control their movements decreases.

There is currently no cure for Parkinson's disease. Symptoms can be controlled in the short term with drugs, deep-brain stimulation, physiotherapy or the implantation of healthy dopamine-producing cells from aborted fetuses.

A recent study of a new treatment showed that adult stem cells could be made to differentiate to replace the dead dopamine-producing nerve cells. The stem cells were removed from a healthy area of each patient's brain and implanted into the area damaged by Parkinson's. Once transplanted, the nerve cells began to differentiate into dopamine-producing cells as hoped. However, the cells then started to die. Unless this death of the new cells can be prevented this treatment is not a permanent cure.

Treatments using embryonic stem cells haven't been tried on humans yet, but there have been good results from studies with rats. In one study, two groups of rats were given a drug that killed the dopamine-producing nerve cells in their brains, giving them a condition like Parkinson's. One group of rats was treated by implanting embryonic stem cells in the damaged area of their brains — the other group weren't treated and were used as a control. The rats' symptoms were studied for nine weeks after treatment. The results are shown on the graph.

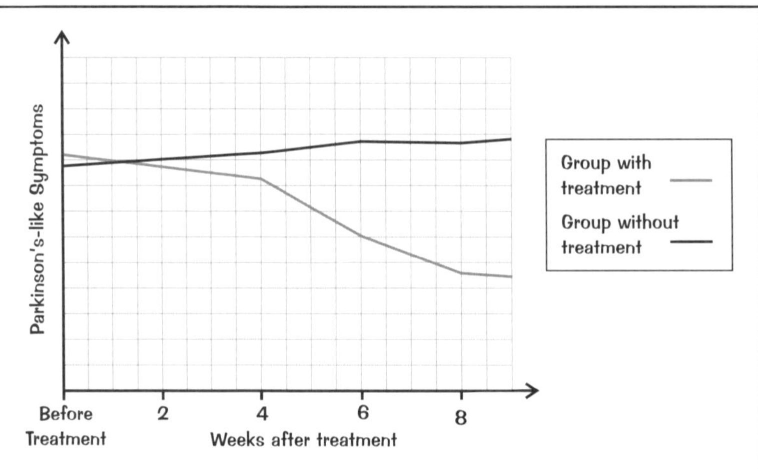

These studies show that more research is needed to realise the potential of stem cells, and that they may well provide a cure for Parkinson's and other diseases in the future.

Stem Cells and Parkinson's

a) Give **three** common symptoms of Parkinson's disease.

....

b) A current treatment for Parkinson's is to transplant brain tissue from fetuses aborted 8 to 12 weeks after conception. Why would these fetuses **not** be suitable for the collection of stem cells?

....

....

c) In the study using embryonic stem cells, the rats were given anti-rejection drugs to stop them rejecting the implanted cells. Why wasn't this needed in the **human** study using **adult** stem cells?

....

....

d) What was the key **problem** found in the human study using adult stem cells to treat Parkinson's? Circle the correct answer.

The patients' immune systems rejected the implanted stem cells.

The stem cells died soon after they were transplanted into the patients' brains.

The stem cells didn't differentiate into the right kind of nerve cell.

The scientists had great difficulty collecting healthy stem cells.

e) The graph in the article shows the level of Parkinson's-like symptoms in the two groups of rats.

i) Compare the level of symptoms in the two groups of rats **before** the treatment.

....

ii) Describe the **trend** in the data from the group of rats given the **stem cell treatment**.

....

....

iii) Which of the following **conclusions** would you draw from the graph? Circle the correct answer.

The treatment eventually cured the treated group of rats of their Parkinson's-like symptoms.

The treatment made the treated group of rats' Parkinson's-like symptoms progressively worse over time.

The treatment was effective in reducing the level of Parkinson's-like symptoms in the group of rats treated.

The treatment would gradually reduce the level of Parkinson's symptoms in humans if used on humans.

Chemicals in the Atmosphere

Q1 The table shows some of the **elements** and **compounds** that are found in **dry air**. Complete the table to show whether the substances are elements or compounds, and give the **chemical symbol** or **formula** for each substance.

substance	element or compound?	symbol
oxygen		
carbon dioxide		
argon		
nitrogen		

Q2 Use the words in the box to complete the passage below. Some words can be used more than once.

molecular **compounds** **weak** **metallic** **atoms** **non-metallic** **strong**

Most .... elements and most compounds formed from .... elements are .... substances. The .... within the molecules are held together by very .... covalent bonds. The forces of attraction between the molecules are very ....

Q3 Complete the following sentences by circling the correct option, and **explain** your answers.

a) The melting and boiling points of simple molecular substances are **low** / **high**.

....

b) Simple molecular substances **conduct** / **don't conduct** electricity.

....

c) Simple molecular substances are usually **gases and liquids** / **solids** at room temperature.

....

Q4 The table gives the **melting** and **boiling points** of some **molecular elements**. State whether each will be a **solid**, **liquid** or **gas** at **room temperature** (25 °C).

element	melting point	boiling point
fluorine	–220 °C	–188 °C
bromine	–7 °C	59 °C
iodine	114 °C	185 °C

a) fluorine ....

b) bromine ....

c) iodine ....

Covalent Bonding

Q1 Indicate whether each statement is **true** or **false**.

a) Covalent bonding involves sharing electrons.

b) Atoms react to gain a full outer shell of electrons.

c) Some atoms can make both ionic and covalent bonds.

d) Hydrogen can form two covalent bonds.

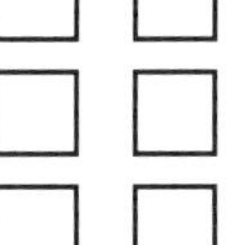

e) Carbon can form four covalent bonds.

"Oi, give me that electron, big nose!"

Q2 Complete the following diagrams by adding **electrons**. Only the **outer shells** are shown.

a) Hydrogen (H_2)

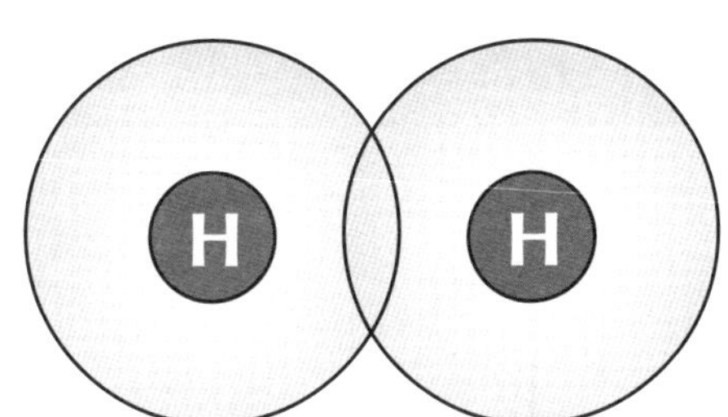

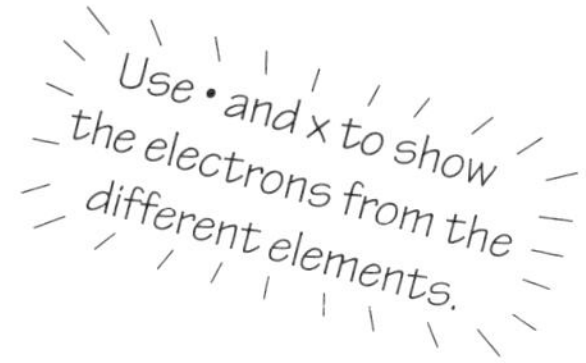

Use • and x to show the electrons from the different elements.

b) Carbon dioxide (CO_2)

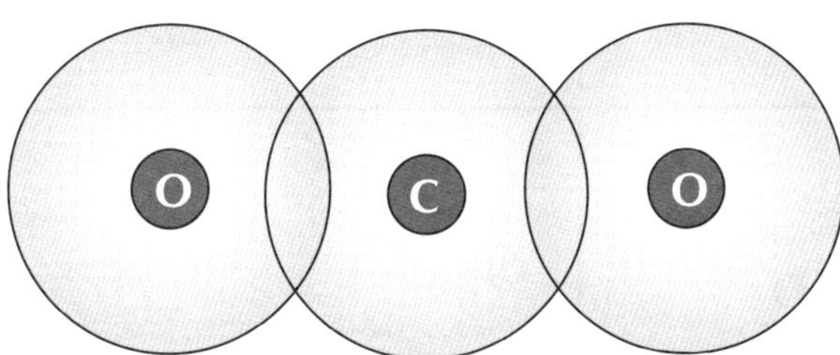

c) Water (H_2O)

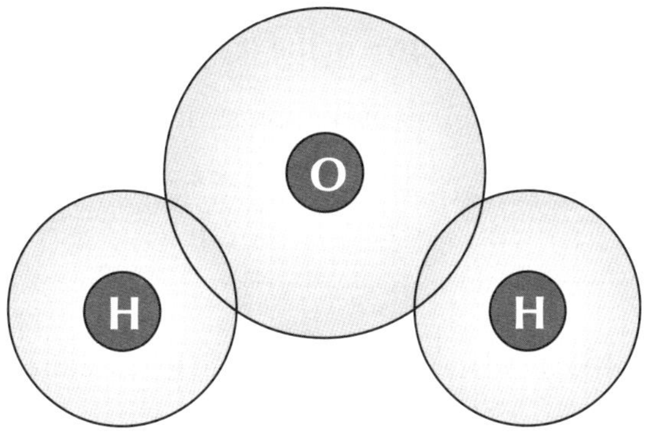

Top Tips: Atoms can bond ionically, as you saw back on page 26, or they can bond covalently. Make sure you know what covalent bonds are, and how they arise. It's really important for understanding all about the chemicals that are floating about up there in the atmosphere.

Covalent Bonding

Q3 Choose from the words in the box to complete the passage below.

electronic	positive	electrostatic	neutral	negative

In a covalent bond, the .... nuclei and the shared .... electrons are held together by .... attraction.

Q4 Complete the table showing the **displayed formulas** and **molecular formulas** of three compounds.

DISPLAYED FORMULA	MOLECULAR FORMULA
H–C–H with H above and below C (H above, H–C–H, H below)	a)
b)	NH_3
O=S=O	c)

Q5 The **displayed formula** of **methane** is shown in the diagram.

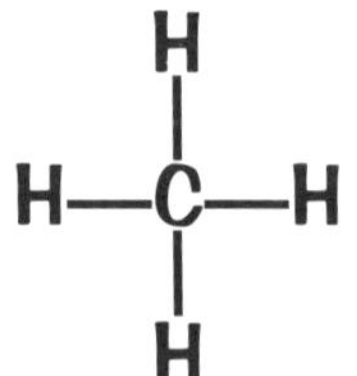

a) What **can't** the displayed formula tell you about the structure of a molecule?

....

....

b) What type of diagram of a methane molecule would give you extra information?

....

Top Tips: There is more than one way of writing a molecule's formula. This isn't just to stop chemists from getting bored — they're all useful for showing different things about the molecule.

Chemicals in the Hydrosphere

Q1 Choose from the words in the box to complete the passage below.

covalent	**salty**	**dissolved**	**water**
ionic	**salts**	**gases**	

The Earth's hydrosphere consists of all the .... on the Earth's surface and the compounds .... in it. Many of these compounds are ...., and are called .... It is these that make seawater ....

Q2 Potassium chloride is an example of a **salt** found in the **sea**. Mike carries out an experiment to find out if **potassium chloride** conducts electricity. He tests the compound when it's **solid** and when it's **dissolved** in water.

a) Complete the following table of results.

	Conducts electricity?
When solid	
When dissolved in water	

b) Explain your answers to part a).

....

....

....

Q3 Sodium chloride has an **ionic structure**.

a) Circle the correct words to explain why sodium chloride has a high melting point.

Sodium chloride has very **strong** / **weak** chemical bonds between the **negative** / **positive** sodium ions and the **negative** / **positive** chloride ions. This means that it needs a **little** / **large** amount of energy to break the bonds.

b) Name two other **properties** of compounds with **ionic structures**.

1. ....

2. ....

Chemicals in the Lithosphere

Q1 Choose from the words in the box to complete the passage describing the Earth's **lithosphere**.

minerals	elements	aluminium	argon	mantle	crust	silicon	oxygen

The .... and part of the .... just below it make up the Earth's lithosphere. It mostly consists of a mixture of ....
..................................., ... and .... are .... found in large amounts in the crust.

Q2 An **abundant** compound in the Earth's lithosphere is **silicon dioxide**.

a) Give **three** properties of silicon dioxide and explain each in terms of its structure.

Property 1: ....

....

Property 2: ....

....

Property 3: ....

....

b) Give **two** types of rock in which silicon dioxide is found in **large quantities**.

....

Q3 Circle the correct words to complete the following paragraph.

Giant covalent structures contain **charged ions / uncharged atoms**.
The covalent bonds between the atoms are **strong / weak**.
Giant covalent structures have **high / low** melting points, they usually **do / don't** conduct electricity and they are usually **soluble / insoluble** in water.

The results suggest a giant covalent structure.

Top Tips: It seems to be all spheres in this section — the atmosphere, the hydrosphere, the lithosphere... Make sure you don't get the facts about them all muddled up. You don't want to be putting the fish up in the sky, or clouds down below the Earth's surface...

Chemicals in the Lithosphere

Q4 The tables below show the **percentage composition** of samples of two different types of **rock**.

Decide which sample is **limestone** and which sample is **sandstone**, and explain your answers.

Sample A	% composition
Si	44.0
O	51.0
Al	0.8
Ca	0.7
Mg	0.1
Other	3.4

Sample B	% composition
Si	1.3
O	47.1
Al	1.6
Ca	38.5
C	11.0
Mg	0.5

Sample A is: ....

Reason: ....

Sample B is: ....

Reason: ....

Q5 Some **minerals** are very valuable as **gemstones**.

a) Explain why some minerals are used as gemstones.

....

b) Why are some gemstones so **valuable**?

....

Q6 **Diamond** is a **giant covalent substance** made entirely from **carbon**.

a) Explain why diamond has a **high melting point**.

....

....

b) Explain how diamond's structure makes it **hard**.

....

....

Top Tips: Examiners just love setting data interpretation questions, and this topic is as good as any for finding one. You might have to interpret data about the amounts of elements in different types of rock, or you might have to apply your knowledge of giant covalent structures to other compounds with this type of structure (such as diamond). Don't worry — it's nothing you can't do.

Chemicals in the Biosphere

Q1 List **six elements** that all **living things** contain.

1. .... 4. ....

2. .... 5. ....

3. .... 6. ....

Q2 The diagram shows the **structural formula** of a **carbohydrate** molecule.
List the **elements** it contains and write its **molecular formula**.

a)

```
HOCH2        O        OH
     \     /   \     /
       C           C
     /  \ H     H /  \
    H    \|     |/    H
          C --- C
          |     |
          OH    OH
```

Elements ....

Molecular formula ....

b) Explain how you can tell that the molecule is a carbohydrate.

....

Q3 The diagram shows the **nitrogen cycle**.

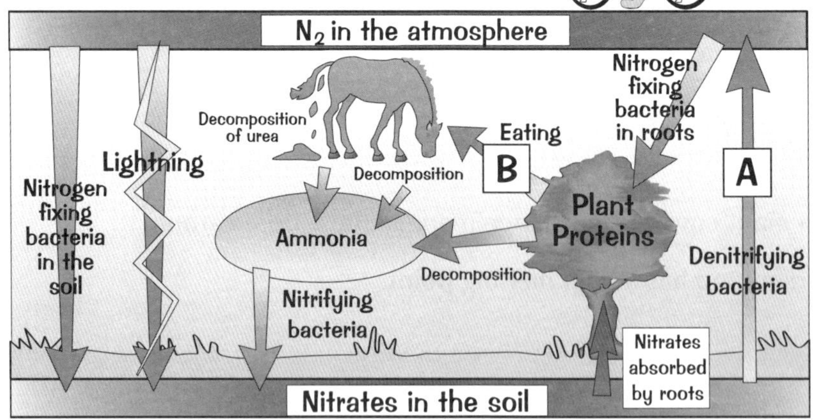

Tick the boxes to show what the labelled arrows represent.

a) Arrow **A** represents:

Denitrifying bacteria moving from the soil to the atmosphere. ☐

Denitrifying bacteria converting nitrates in the soil into nitrogen in the atmosphere. ☐

b) Arrow **B** represents:

Nitrogen from plants moving into animals by feeding. ☐

Nitrogen being released into the atmosphere through feeding. ☐

Metals from Minerals

Q1 Indicate whether each of the statements below about **metal ores** is true or false.

		True	False
a)	Ores are rocks containing minerals from which metals can be extracted.	☐	☐
b)	The more reactive the metal, the easier it is to extract from its ore.	☐	☐
c)	Zinc, iron and copper can all be extracted by heating their ores with carbon monoxide.	☐	☐
d)	When a metal oxide loses oxygen, it is reduced.	☐	☐

Q2 **Copper** may have first been extracted when someone accidentally dropped some copper ore into a **wood fire**. When the ashes were cleared away some copper was left.

a) Explain how dropping copper ore into a fire could lead to the extraction of copper.

....

b) Why do you think that copper was one of the first metals to be extracted from its ore?

....

Q3 Fill in the blanks in the passage below about **extracting metals** from their **ores**.

> .... is often used to extract metals that are
> .... it in the reactivity series. Oxygen is removed
> from a metal oxide in a process called ....
> Other metals have to be extracted using ....
> because they are .... reactive.

You'll find a periodic table helpful for these questions.

Q4 Dave is **calculating** how much **metal** can be **extracted** from certain ores.

a) Calculate the mass of iron that can be extracted from 500 g iron oxide (Fe_2O_3).

....

....

b) Could more metal be obtained from the same mass of copper oxide (CuO)?

....

....

Top Tips: Metals aren't usually found in the ground as pure lumps. They need to be extracted from their ores, and this is done by a variety of methods. The ones you need to know about are reduction using carbon and electrolysis. Which is what these pages are all about...

Electrolysis

Q1 Complete the passage about **electrolysis** using words from the box below.

dissolved	molecules	electric	given to	electrolyte
decompose	external circuit	taken from	molten	

During the electrolysis of an ionic compound, an .... current is passed through a .... or .... substance, causing it to .... Electrons are .... ions at the positive electrode and are passed through the .... to the negative electrode, where they are .... other ions in the solution. Atoms or .... are formed.

Q2 The diagram below shows the electrolysis of **molten aluminium oxide**.

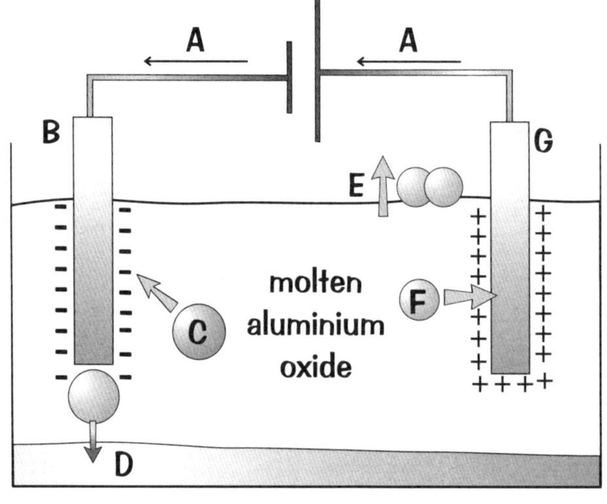

Write the labels that should go at points A–G:

A ....

B ....

C ....

D ....

E ....

F ....

G ....

Q3 Explain why the **electrolyte** needs to be either a **solution** or **molten** for electrolysis to work.

....

....

Electrolysis

Q4 a) Tick the correct boxes to show whether the following statements are **true** or **false**.

	True	False
i) Ionic substances can only be electrolysed if molten or in solution.	☐	☐
ii) In the extraction of aluminium the electrolyte is molten aluminium metal.	☐	☐
iii) The aluminium produced is molten.	☐	☐
iv) Aluminium ions gain electrons in electrolysis.	☐	☐
v) Aluminium is formed at the positive electrode.	☐	☐

b) Write out a correct version of each false statement.

....

....

....

....

Q5 **Aluminium** is the most **abundant** metal in the Earth's crust.

Goodness, how awfully common... ooo

a) **i)** Circle the correct word:

The most common aluminium ore is <u>bauxite / cryolite</u>.

ii) When this ore is mined and purified, which compound is obtained? Give its name and formula.

Name .... **Formula** ....

b) Why can't aluminium be extracted by **reduction** with carbon?

....

c) Although it's very common, aluminium was not discovered until about 200 years ago. Suggest why.

....

Q6 **Aluminium** is extracted from its ore by **electrolysis**.

Write balanced half-equations for the reactions at the electrodes.

Negative electrode: ....

Positive electrode: ....

Top Tips: Usually, things that are common are cheap to buy — like potatoes. But, even though aluminium is as common a metal as you're going to get, it's not actually that cheap because it costs a lot to extract. (Potatoes, on the other hand, are easy to extract — just get digging.)

Metals

Q1 The table shows the **properties** of **four elements** found in the periodic table.

ELEMENT	MELTING POINT (°C)	DENSITY (g/cm^3)	ELECTRICAL CONDUCTIVITY
A	1084	8.9	Excellent
B	–39	13.6	Very good
C	3500	3.51	Very poor
D	1536	7.87	Very good

a) Which **three** of the above elements are most likely to be **metals**?

....

b) Explain how you know the other element is **not** a metal.

....

....

Q2 This table shows some of the **properties** of four different **metals**.

Metal	Heat conduction	Cost	Resistance to corrosion	Strength
1	average	high	excellent	good
2	average	medium	good	excellent
3	excellent	low	good	good
4	low	high	average	poor

Some metal is heavy.

Use the information in the table to choose which metal would be **best** for making:

a) Saucepan bases ....

b) Car bodies ....

c) A statue for a town centre ....

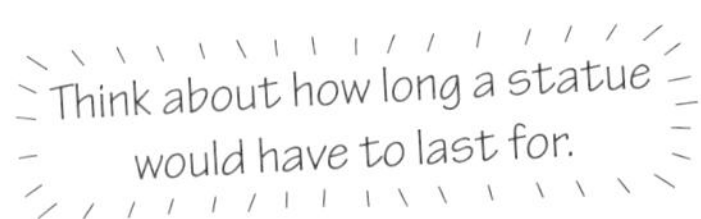

Think about how long a statue
would have to last for.

Q3 Complete the following sentences about metals.

a) Metals have a giant .... structure.

b) Metals are good conductors of .... and ....

c) The atoms in metals can slide over each other, so metals are ....

Metals

Q4 All metals have a similar **structure**. This explains why many of them have similar **properties**.

a) Draw a labelled diagram of a typical metal structure, showing the electrons.

b) What is unusual about the electrons in a metal?

....

Q5 Complete the following sentences by choosing from the words in the box.

Each word should only be used once (or not at all).

hammered	**weak**	**low**	**high**	**strong**	**malleable**	**folded**

a) Metals have a .... tensile strength.

b) Metals are .... and hard to break.

c) Metals can be .... into different shapes because they are ....

Q6 Explain how **electricity** is conducted through metals.

....

....

Q7 Explain why most metals have **high melting points**.

....

....

Top Tip: Okay, so metals form weird bonds. The electrons can go wandering about through the material, and it's this that gives them some of their characteristic properties. It's pretty important that you learn the key phrases that examiners like — 'giant structure', 'sea of free electrons', etc.

Environmental Impact

Q1 Ores are **finite resources**.

a) Explain what finite resources are.

....

....

b) Explain why it is a **problem** that ores are finite resources.
Suggest one thing that can be done to **reduce** this problem.

....

....

Q2 New **mines** always have **social**, **economic** and **environmental** consequences. Complete this table by putting **two** more effects that a new mine can have in each of the columns.

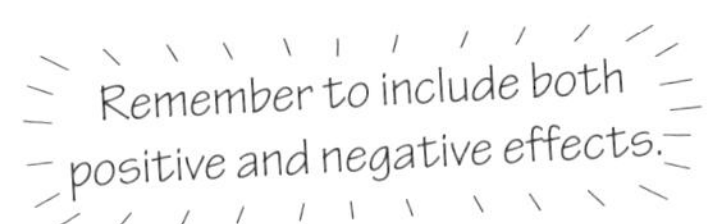
Remember to include both
positive and negative effects.

Social	Economic	Environmental
Services, e.g. Healthcare may be improved because of influx of people.		Pollution from traffic.

Top Tips: It's important to be able to weigh up the issues surrounding the extraction of metals. There are plenty of positive and negative effects of mining, so make sure you've got them sorted here so that you don't have to spend loads of time thinking if they come up in the exam.

Environmental Impact

Q3 Read the article below and answer the questions that follow.

Metals play a major role in modern life. However, none of the stages in the life cycle of a metal product are free from environmental problems.

Mining

Although mining brings money and employment, which have a positive impact on the development of an area, there are plenty of negatives. Mining destroys landscapes and habitats, produces waste products and causes noise pollution. Transporting the ore takes energy and causes pollution.

Extraction

Extracting pure metal from the ore is also not without problems. Non-renewable resources, such as fossil fuels, are usually used to provide the energy needed to extract the metals. This in turn leads to air pollution, which has its own problems such as acid rain and climate change.

Use

Metals are often used for products which have an impact on the environment. Take, for example, cars — they burn non-renewable fuels and produce pollution.

Disposal

At the end of their life, metals are often disposed of in landfill sites. These are unattractive and some metals can be dangerous if disposed of in this way. Vehicles accessing the sites cause pollution, dust and noise.

One answer to these problems is recycling. Take aluminium — it can be recycled over and over again without losing any of its properties in the process. The process doesn't take long either — recycled aluminium cans are usually back on the shelves within eight weeks.

In the UK, it's estimated that we use about 5 billion aluminium cans every year. In 2001, 42% of these cans were recycled (up from 31% of cans used in 1996).

Recycling aluminium uses only 5% of the energy needed to extract pure aluminium from bauxite, and produces only 5% of the carbon dioxide emissions.

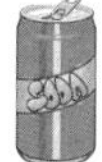

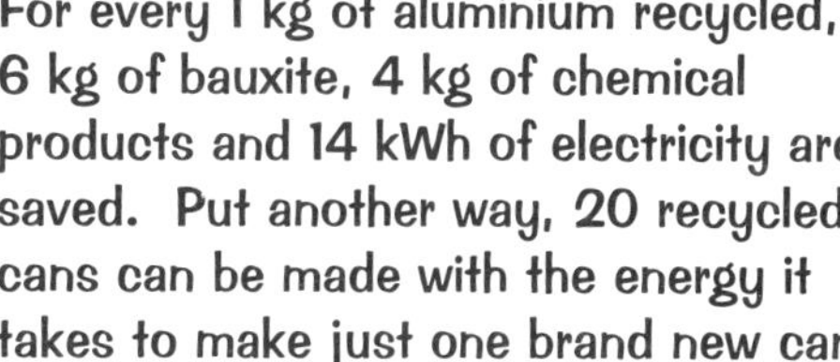

For every 1 kg of aluminium recycled, 6 kg of bauxite, 4 kg of chemical products and 14 kWh of electricity are saved. Put another way, 20 recycled cans can be made with the energy it takes to make just one brand new can.

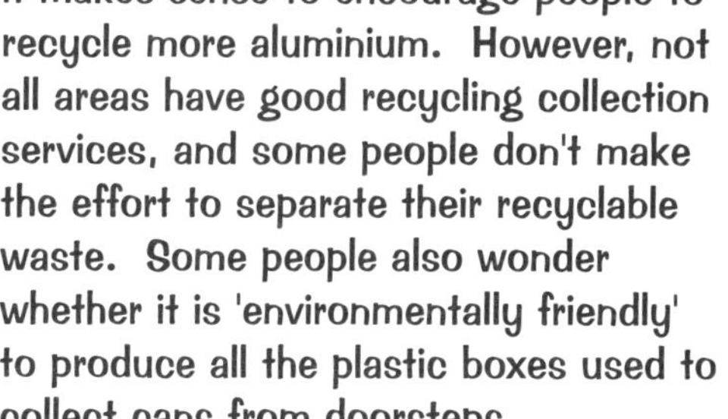

The use of aluminium is rising quickly so it makes sense to encourage people to recycle more aluminium. However, not all areas have good recycling collection services, and some people don't make the effort to separate their recyclable waste. Some people also wonder whether it is 'environmentally friendly' to produce all the plastic boxes used to collect cans from doorsteps.

Environmental Impact

a) Give two **environmental problems** associated with the mining of metal ores.

....

....

b) Describe one **benefit** that an aluminium ore mine can have for the local area.

....

c) How can the use of metals cause environmental problems **indirectly**?

....

d) Suggest why it is a good thing that aluminium does not lose its properties during the recycling process.

....

e) By how much did the percentage of aluminium cans recycled increase between **1996** and **2001**?

....

f) The article states that about 5 billion aluminium cans are used every year in the UK. How many cans were **recycled** in **2001**?

....

g) State **two** reasons that people might give for not recycling their aluminium packaging.

....

....

h) Select one sentence or phrase from the article that demonstrates that recycling aluminium is very energy efficient.

....

....

i) Give **one** problem that could be associated with the use of kerbside recycling boxes.

....

....

Static Electricity

Q1 Fill in the gaps in these sentences with the words in the box.

electrons	positive	static	friction	insulating	negative

.... electricity can build up when two .... materials are rubbed together. The .... causes .... to be transferred from one material onto the other. This leaves a .... charge on one of the materials and a .... charge on the other.

Q2 **Circle** the pairs of charges that would **attract** each other and **underline** those that would **repel**.

positive and positive   positive and negative   negative and positive   negative and negative

Q3 Tick the boxes to show whether the following statements are **true** or **false**.

		True	False
a)	Electrons are negatively charged particles.	☐	☐
b)	Areas of positive charge are caused by the movement of positive charges.	☐	☐
c)	Negatively charged areas occur because electrons are attracted to each other.	☐	☐

Q4 Three friends are talking about some of the **effects** of static electricity.

Lisa: Why does my hair sometimes stick out and cling to the brush?

Sara: Why is the TV screen always dusty — my mum cleans it all the time?

Tim: Why do I hear a crackling sound when I take off my shirt?

Answer their questions in terms of the attraction and repulsion between **charges**.

Lisa: ....

....

Sara: ....

....

Tim: ....

....

Top Tips: Static electricity's responsible for many of life's little irritations — bad hair days, and those little shocks you get from touching car doors and even stroking the cat.

Electric Current

Q1 Complete the following sentences by choosing the **correct** words from the box.

flow	voltage	resistance	charge	ohms	current	force	amperes

a) Current is the .... of .... round a circuit.

b) .... acts like a .... that pushes the current round the circuit.

c) .... restricts the flow of current round the circuit.

Q2 Connect each **quantity** with the name and symbol of its **unit**.

A	Current	volts
V	Resistance	amperes
Ω	Voltage	ohms

Q3 Tick the boxes to show whether the following statements are **true** or **false**.

		True	False
a)	Conventional current flows from negative to positive.	☐	☐
b)	A component, such as a lamp or motor, resists the flow of charge through it.	☐	☐
c)	Electrons flow from negative to positive.	☐	☐
d)	The wires in an electric circuit are full of charges that are fixed in place.	☐	☐

Q4 The flow of electricity in circuits can be compared to the flow of **water in pipes**.

a) "The pipes in a water 'circuit' are full of water that is free to move."
What is the equivalent of this statement for an electrical circuit?

....

....

b) What electrical device does the **pump** in the water 'circuit' correspond to? ....

c) The system in the diagram has a **constriction** where it is harder for the water to flow.
What corresponds to this constriction in an electrical circuit?

....

d) The pump is **turned up**. What would the equivalent action be in an electrical circuit?

....

Electric Current

Q5 The **current** that flows in a circuit is determined by the sizes of the forces pushing it and opposing it.

World's Strongest Current

a) Describe how the voltage of the battery affects the size of the current that will flow.

....

b) Without changing the battery, how could the current be:

i) increased? ....

ii) decreased? ....

Q6 **Electric wires** are usually made of a **metal**, such as copper, covered in an **insulating** material.

a) Why are insulators unable to conduct electricity?

....

b) Why are metals able to conduct electricity?

....

c) What particles move when current flows in a metallic conductor?

....

Q7 Ranjit makes the **electric circuit** shown in the diagram. The **lamp lights** up, but when Ranjit **opens** the switch it **goes out**. He discusses why this happens with his friends.

Lara says, "When the switch is open, charge leaks out and so doesn't reach the lamp."

Brian says, "All the charge must have been used up when the switch was closed."

Ranjit says, "The circuit is not complete when the switch is open so no current flows."

a) Which person has the correct explanation? ....

b) Explain why the other two people are incorrect.

....

....

....

....

Circuits — The Basics

Q1 Match up these items from a standard test circuit with the **correct description** and **symbol**.

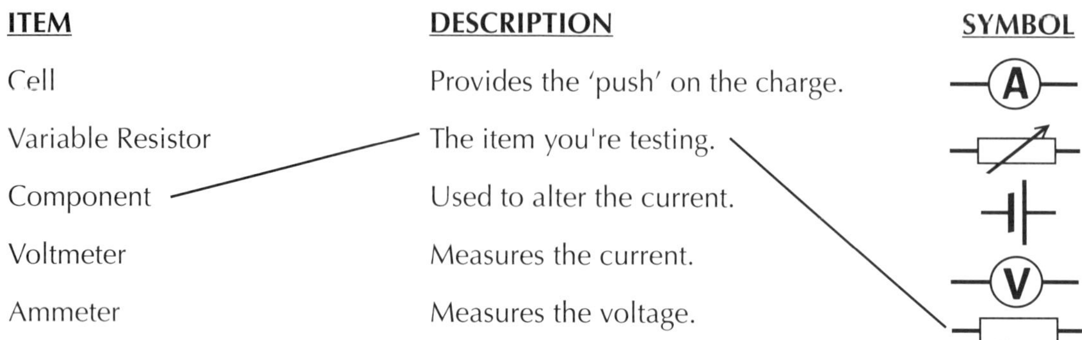

ITEM	DESCRIPTION	SYMBOL
Cell	Provides the 'push' on the charge.	A
Variable Resistor	The item you're testing.	
Component	Used to alter the current.	
Voltmeter	Measures the current.	V
Ammeter	Measures the voltage.	

Q2 The diagram below shows a **complete circuit**.

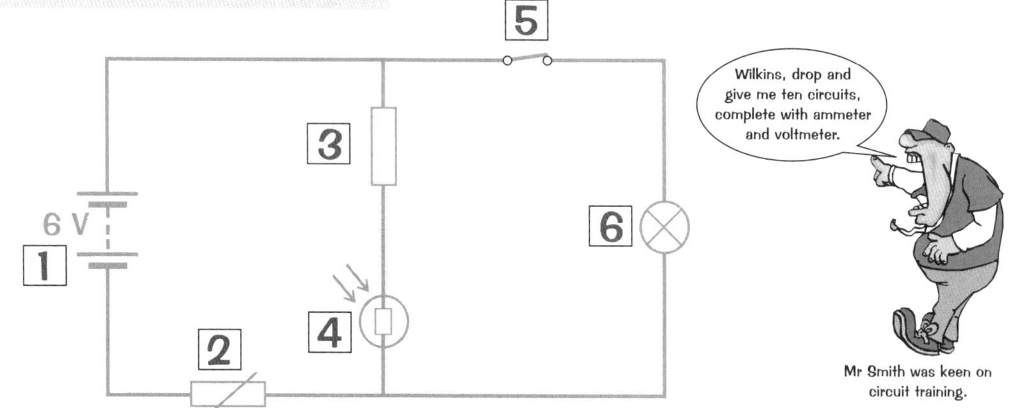
5
3
6 V
1
6
4
2
Wilkins, drop and give me ten circuits, complete with ammeter and voltmeter.

Mr Smith was keen on circuit training.

a) Give the name of each of the numbered components.

1. .... 2. .... 3. ....

4. .... 5. .... 6. ....

b) Draw an **ammeter** on the circuit in the correct position to measure the current leaving the battery.

c) Draw a **voltmeter** on the circuit in the correct position to measure the voltage across the lamp.

Q3 Complete the following passage by choosing the correct words from the box. Each word may be used once, more than once, or not at all.

charge	voltmeter	battery	potential difference	current
parallel	energy	series	components	

Voltage (or ....) measures how much .... is transferred to or from the .... as it moves between two points. The .... transfers .... to the charge and .... transfer it away from the charge. A .... must be connected in ....

Resistance

Q1 The graph below shows **V-I curves** for four **resistors**.

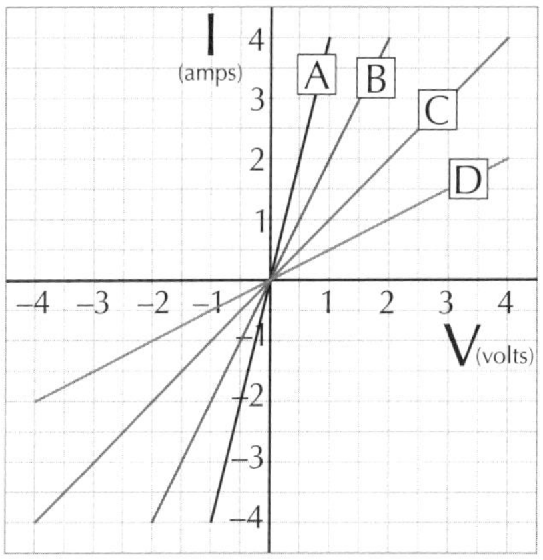

Gradient = $\frac{\text{vertical change}}{\text{horizontal change}}$

a) Which resistor has the **highest** resistance? ....

b) Calculate the gradient of the line for **resistor B**.

....

c) Calculate the resistance of resistor B.

....

Q2 Tick the boxes to show whether the following statements are **true** or **false**.

		True	False
a)	LDRs and thermistors are types of **variable** resistor.	☐	☐
b)	An LDR has a **high** resistance in very **bright** light.	☐	☐
c)	The resistance of a thermistor **increases** as the temperature **decreases**.	☐	☐
d)	An LDR could be part of a useful thermostat.	☐	☐

Q3 Leyla was doing her homework when the **light** on her desk **went out**. Leyla's mum says the **bulb** has blown and needs replacing, but that they should wait till it **cools down** before touching it.

a) What causes the filament in the lamp to get hot when current passes through it?

....

....

b) Why are the filaments in lamps designed to have a very high resistance?

....

Q4 Fill in the missing values in the table on the right.

Use a formula triangle to help.

Voltage (V)	Current (A)	Resistance (Ω)
6	2	
8		2
	3	3
4	8	
2		4
	0.5	2

Resistance

Q5 Peter's teacher has given him an unlabelled **resistor**. Peter plans an experiment to **work out** its **resistance** but he is worried that the resistance of the **wires** in his test circuit will affect his results.

a) **i)** What is normally assumed about the resistance of the wires in a circuit?

....

ii) Why would this assumption be unlikely to make Peter's results inaccurate?

....

b) Peter plans to vary the current through the resistor and take several pairs of voltage-current readings. He will work out the resistance for each pair of readings, then calculate an average.

i) What happens to the temperature of a resistor when current flows through it?

....

ii) Explain why Peter should try to keep his test resistor at a constant temperature.

....

Q6 Miriam is testing **three components** (A, B and C) using a standard test circuit. She knows that component A is a fixed resistor, but doesn't know what components B and C are.

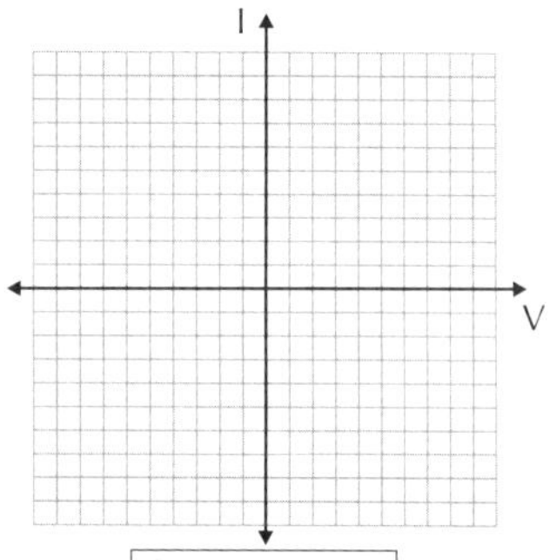

a) Sketch a graph on the axes on the right to show how the current through **component A** would vary with voltage.

Component A

b) While Miriam was testing **component B**, her friend Lakisha **opened the blinds** covering the windows. The graph below shows Miriam's results. Lakisha opened the blinds at the point marked 'X' on the graph.

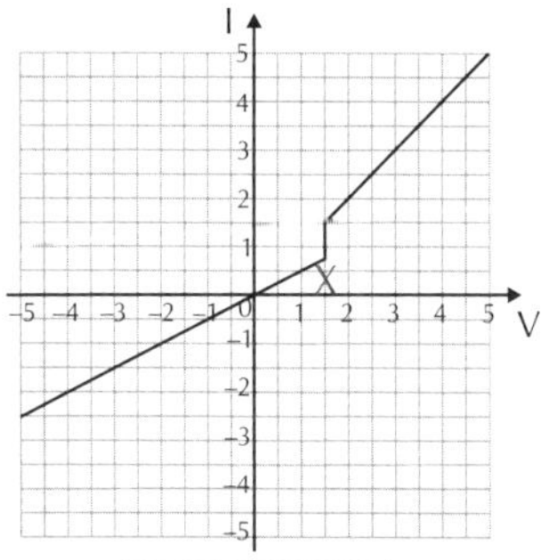

Component B

i) What effect did opening the blinds have on the **resistance** of component B?

....

....

ii) What might component B be? ....

c) **Component C** is used as part of a **thermostat** and its resistance changes according to the temperature.

i) What is component C? ....

ii) Describe how the resistance of component C will change as it is gradually warmed.

....

....

Top Tips: There are two very important skills you need to master for resistance questions — **interpreting V-I graphs** and using the formula **V = I × R**. Make sure you can do both.

Series Circuits

Q1 Match up these **descriptions** with what they describe in a **series circuit**.

Same everywhere in the circuit

Shared by all the components

The sum of the resistances

Can be different for each component

Potential difference

Current

Total potential difference

Total resistance

Q2 The diagram shows a series circuit.

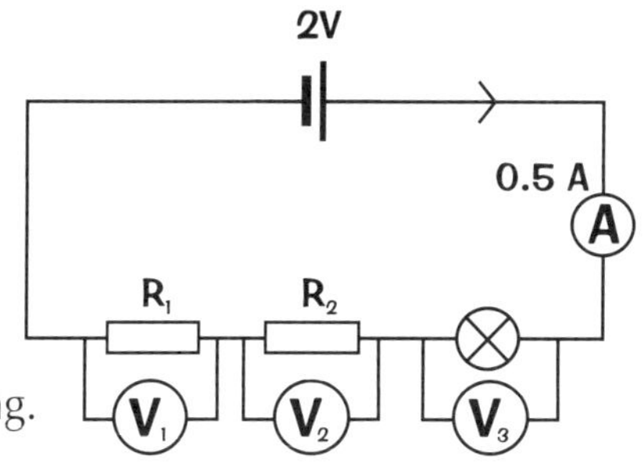

2V

0.5 A

A

R_1 R_2

V_1 V_2 V_3

a) What component could be added to the circuit to **increase** the voltage and current?

....

b) Voltmeter V_1 has the lowest reading and V_3 has the highest reading.

i) Which component has the **highest** resistance? ....

ii) What does this tell you about the energy transferred to each component?

....

c) Why is the **total resistance** of the circuit greater than the resistance of any one of the components?

....

Q3 Vikram does an experiment with different numbers of **lamps** in two **series circuits**. The diagram on the right shows his two circuits.

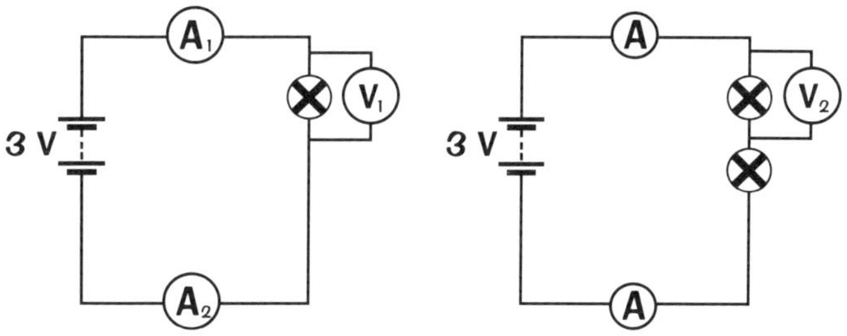

A_1 V_1 3 V A_2

A V_2 3 V A

a) The reading on ammeter A_1 in the first circuit is 0.2 A.

i) What is the reading on ammeter A_2? ....

ii) How do you know this? ....

b) Vikram is puzzled because the two voltmeters show different readings even though all the lamps are the same.

i) Which voltmeter shows the **higher** reading? ....

ii) Explain, in terms of energy, why the voltage across the lamps is different for each circuit.

....

....

Parallel Circuits

Q1 Tick to show whether these statements about parallel circuits are **true** or **false**.

		True	False
a)	Components are connected separately to the power supply.	☐	☐
b)	Each component has the same potential difference across it.	☐	☐
c)	Components can be switched on and off independently.	☐	☐

Q2 Karen does an experiment with different numbers of identical **lamps** in three **parallel circuits**. The diagrams on the right show her three circuits.

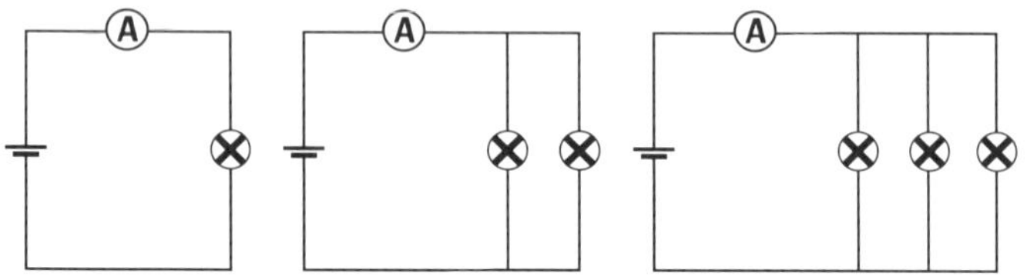

Explain what happens to the following quantities when **more lamps** are added.

a) The **voltage** across each lamp. ....

....

b) The **current** passing through each lamp. ....

....

c) The **resistance** of each lamp. ....

....

Q3 The diagram opposite shows a **parallel** circuit. Ammeter A_2 has a reading of **0.27 A** and A_3 has a reading of **0.43 A**.

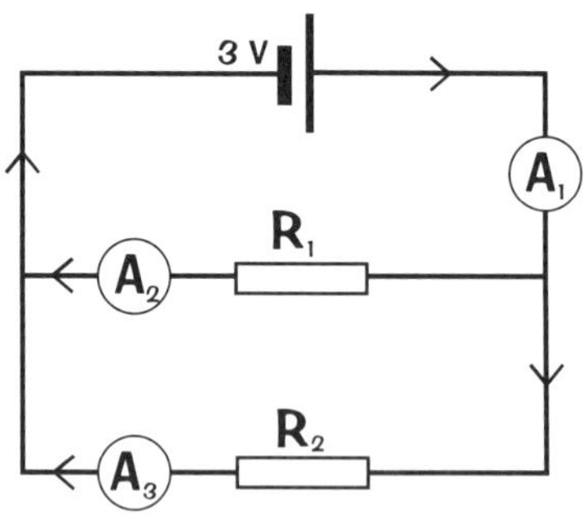

a) i) What reading is shown on ammeter A_1? ....

ii) Explain your answer. ....

....

b) i) Which resistor has the **smallest** resistance? Explain your answer.

....

....

ii) Will the **total** resistance be larger, smaller or equal to the resistance of this resistor? Why?

....

....

c) Resistor R_2 is removed from the circuit. What is the new reading on ammeter A_2?

....

Mains Electricity

Q1 **Mains electricity** is distributed around the country by the **National Grid**.

a) At what **voltage** is mains electricity supplied to people's homes?

....

b) What is the difference between the current supplied by a **battery** and mains electricity?

....

c) What is the name of the process that generators use to produce electricity?

....

Q2 Inga is experimenting with a **magnet** and a **coil of wire**. When she moves the north pole of the magnet **into** the coil, a **positive** voltage is induced.

a) In which direction will the induced voltage be if Inga:

i) Moves the magnet back out of the coil? ....

ii) Reverses the magnet's north-south polarity, then moves it into the coil in the same way as before? ....

b) Explain what will happen if Inga:

i) Holds the magnet still inside the coil.

....

ii) Sets up her apparatus so that the magnet moves repeatedly into and out of the coil.

....

Q3 Use the words in the box to **fill in the blanks** in this paragraph about generating electricity.

moving electromagnetic magnet coil induction alternating voltage reverses magnetic complete

You can create a .... across an electrical conductor by .... a magnet near the conductor. This is called .... In simple generators, this is usually achieved by rotating a .... near a .... of wire. The generator produces a(n) .... current when it is connected up to a .... circuit.

Mains Electricity

Q4 A simple **generator** can be made by rotating a magnet inside a coil of wire.

a) When the magnet turns half a turn, what happens to:

i) The magnetic field? ....

ii) The voltage across the coil? ....

b) The magnet is spun in one direction. Does this generate an **AC** or **DC** current in the wire?

....

c) Mains electricity is supplied as alternating current. Explain why this is used.

....

Q5 Look at the simple **generators** sketched below.

A ☐ Coil spread over greater area

B ☐ Quicker rotation

C ☐ More coils

D ☐ Stronger magnet

One of the generators labelled A - D will **not** induce a higher voltage than the generator in the blue box. Tick the appropriate box.

Q6 The diagram shows a **hamster-powered generator**.

a) What happens in the coil of wire when the hamster runs at a **constant speed**? Explain your answer.

....

....

....

b) What would change if the hamster ran in the **opposite direction** (at the same speed as before)?

....

c) Meg wants to use the generator to charge her mobile phone, which requires a **12 V** electrical supply. The generator supplies **2 V** to the primary coil of a transformer which has **24 turns**. How many turns must there be on the **secondary coil**?

....

Mains Electricity

Q7 Number the following statements in the right order to explain how a transformer works.

	This causes a rapidly-changing magnetic field in the core.
	An alternating current can flow in a circuit connected to the secondary coil.
	An alternating current flows in the primary coil.
1	An alternating voltage is connected to the primary coil of a transformer.
	The changing magnetic field induces an alternating voltage in the secondary coil.

Q8 Transformers have a **laminated iron core**.

a) Describe the structure of a transformer.

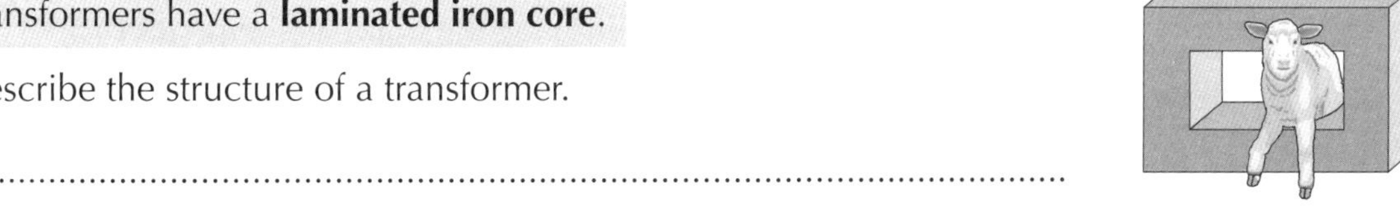

....

....

b) What is the difference between a **step-up** and a **step-down** transformer?

....

....

c) Why do transformers work with **alternating** current **only**?

....

....

Q9 Use the **transformer equation** to complete the following table.

Number of turns on primary coil	Voltage to primary coil (V)	Number of turns on secondary coil	Voltage to secondary coil (V)
1000	12	4000	
1000		2000	20
1000	12		12
	33 000	500	230

Top Tips: Electromagnetic induction is a very **useful** bit of Physics, because it's how we make all our electricity. The massive generators in a power station work like this — there's a **conductor** experiencing a **changing magnetic field**, and the result is an **induced voltage**.

Electrical Energy

Q1 Fill in the gaps using the words in the box. You might need to use some of the words more than once, or not at all.

power	current	energy	from	to	transfers	produces	voltage

When electric charge flows through an appliance .... is transferred .... the appliance. The power of an appliance is the rate at which it .... from the charge passing through it.

Q2 Calculate the **amount** of electrical energy transferred by the following **appliances**.

a) A 100 watt lamp in 10 seconds: ....

b) A 500 watt motor in 2 minutes: ....

c) A 1 kW heater in 20 seconds: ....

Don't forget to use the right units.

Q3 Joanna is going to sell **tea and cakes** after a school concert to raise money for charity. She has found the **cost** of all the **ingredients**, but now needs to calculate the **electricity** costs so she can work out how much to charge people.

a) The water boiler in the school canteen takes 36 minutes to boil when full and is rated at 2.2 kW. Calculate the energy transferred, in kilowatt-hours, by the water boiler when it boils the water.

....

b) The water boiler can keep water hot using 150 joules of energy per second. Joanna estimates they will need to keep the water hot for 25 minutes. How much energy will be transferred in this time?

....

c) The school oven has a power of 2.7 kW and will be on for 1 hour and 15 minutes to bake the cakes. How much energy will be transferred in this time?

....

d) The electricity company charges 8.5p per kilowatt-hour.

i) How much electrical energy will Joanna use in total? ....

ii) How much will this cost? ....

Q4 Rory and Ellouise are trying to work out whose **remote-controlled car** has **more power**.

a) Calculate the power of each car.

i) Rory's car transfers 2700 J of energy in 50 seconds. ....

ii) Ellouise's car transfers 3400 J of energy in 1 minute 10 seconds. ....

b) Whose car has the greater power? ....

Electrical Energy

Q5 Simon and Polly are discussing the units of **energy** and **power**.

Simon says, "Energy is measured in kilowatt-hours — just like on an electricity bill."
Polly says, "That's wrong, energy is always measured in joules — kilowatt-hours measure power."

a) Who is right? Explain your answer.

....

....

b) Why are there two units for electrical energy?

....

Q6 Lucy is comparing **three lamps**. She connects each lamp in a circuit and measures the **current**. Her results are shown in the table below.

Complete the table by filling in the missing values.

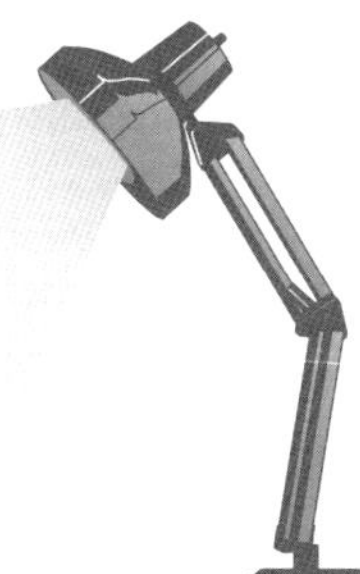

	Lamp A	Lamp B	Lamp C
Voltage (V)	12		
Current (A)	2.5	4	0.1
Power (W)		12	
Energy used in one minute (J)			1380

Q7 Here is an **energy flow diagram** for an electric lamp. Complete the following sentences.

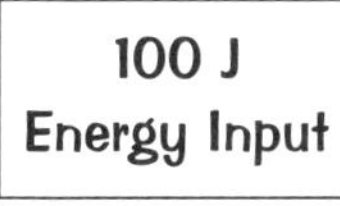

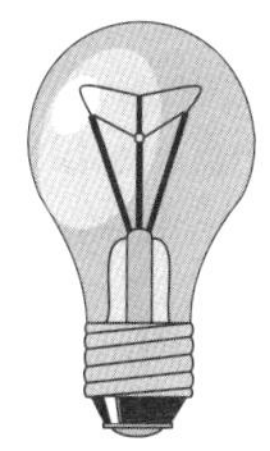

a) The **total energy supplied** is .... J

b) The **energy usefully transferred** is .... J

c) The amount of energy **wasted** is .... J

d) The **efficiency** of the lamp is .... %

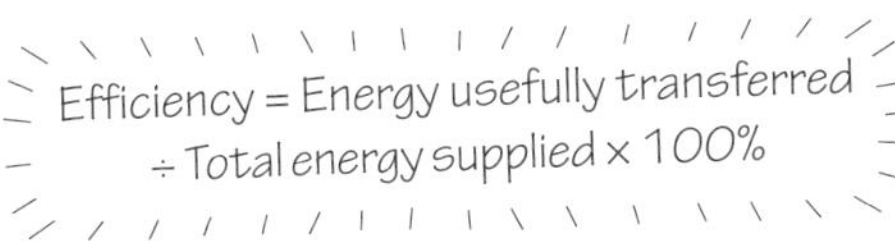

Q8 Use the **efficiency formula** to complete the table.

Total Energy Supplied (J)	Energy Usefully Transferred (J)	Efficiency (%)
2000	1500	
	2000	50
4000		25
600	200	

The National Grid

Q1 Read the passage below and answer the questions that follow.

National Grid Celebrates 75th Birthday

2008 marks the 75th year since the National Grid began operation. The National Grid is the network of cables and pylons that distributes electricity throughout the UK. The idea of a national grid was proposed by Lord Weir in 1925, as a solution to the inefficient and fragmented electricity supply system in operation at that time.

In the early 20th century most of the demand for electricity was for lighting in the homes of the few who could afford it. However, with developments in the technology used to generate AC electricity large power stations began to be built. This decreased the cost of electricity meaning that it was affordable for more people to use at home and cost-effective for industry.

As more and more people started to use electricity problems began to occur. The supply systems often struggled to meet demand — supply would stop altogether or become patchy and unreliable. Another problem was that different power stations supplied electricity at different voltages, which meant that people could only use certain lamps and appliances.

The solution to these problems was the National Grid, which began operating in 1933 as a set of local grids. In 1938 these grids were connected to form the single system we know today. Construction of the National Grid had an enormous impact on the number of houses with an electricity supply — 65% of all houses in the UK were connected by 1938. By 1948, 85% of houses were connected and electricity was no longer the luxury it had once been.

The National Grid revolutionised electricity distribution in the UK, and 75 years on is still going strong. However, it's not particularly efficient (wasting around 30 000 GWh* every year) and the high-voltage power cables across the country can be dangerous and have even been linked with leukaemia.

The method used to maximise the efficiency of the system is to use transformers to distribute electricity with a high voltage (400 000 V) and low current. This allows high power to be transmitted and minimises the heating effect caused by the flow of current, reducing the energy wasted as heat.

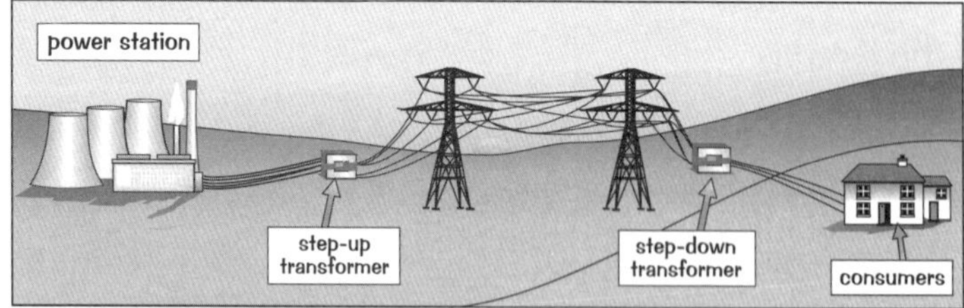

As a country, we rely on the National Grid so much that it is difficult to imagine a future without it in one form or another. Scientists are currently researching alternative methods of transmission, including beaming energy from solar power satellites or using superconducting resistance-free cables to end power losses and improve the Grid.

* 1 GWh = 1 000 000 kWh

The National Grid

a) Suggest **two** ways in which the development of the National Grid benefited society.

....

....

....

....

b) In the late 19th century, DC was safer than AC and could be stored. However, when large-scale generation and distribution became an issue, AC power stations were chosen in preference to DC ones. Suggest a reason for this.

....

....

c) Use the equation **Power = Potential Difference × Current** to calculate the current flowing in the high-voltage distribution cables when 70 MW of electricity is distributed. (1MW = 1 000 000 W)

....

d) The voltage of electricity is stepped up before transmission using a transformer.

i) Complete the labels on the diagram of a transformer.

1. ....

2. ....

3. ....

4. ....

ii) A power station generates electricity at 25 000 V. The supply needs to be stepped up to 400 000 V for transmission. If this was done using a single transformer with 50 turns on its primary coil, how many turns would be needed on the secondary coil?

....

....

e) The National Grid supplies approximately 370 000 GWh of energy a year to homes and industry. Calculate its efficiency.

....

f) Explain why 'superconducting resistance-free cables' would minimise power lost from the cables.

....

....

The Nervous System

Q1 Complete the following passage using words from the box.

environment favourable change mate
stimulus respond temperature danger

A .... is any .... in the ....
of an organism, for example a change in air .... It's important
that organisms .... to stimuli to keep themselves in
.... conditions, for example to avoid ....
or when finding a ....

Q2 The **CNS** makes up part of the **nervous system**.

a) What do the letters **CNS** stand for?

....

b) What is the **function** of the CNS?

....

c) On the diagram label the parts that make up the CNS.

d) What is the role of the **peripheral** nervous system?

....

....

e) What type of neurones:

i) carry information **to** the CNS? ....

ii) carry instructions **from** the CNS? ....

Q3 Complete the diagram below to show the pathway of information through the nervous system.

Stimulus						Response

The Nervous System

Q4 Jamie was cooking his mum some tea when he accidentally picked up a **hot** saucepan. Jamie **instantly** dropped the pan back onto the hob.

Put numbers in the boxes so that the following statements are in the correct order to describe how Jamie's nervous system responded to him picking up the hot pan. The first one has been done for you.

- [ ] Some of the muscles in Jamie's hand contract, causing him to drop the pan.
- [1] Temperature receptors in Jamie's hand detect the increase in temperature.
- [ ] Impulses travel along a motor neurone.
- [ ] Impulses travel along a sensory neurone.
- [ ] The information is processed by the spinal cord.

Q5 **Receptors** and **effectors** are important cells in the nervous system.

a) What is the role of effectors?

....

b) What are receptors?

....

c) Put the words below into the correct columns in the table to show the different types of effectors and receptors, and the different **organs** they form part of.

sound receptor cells ~~taste buds~~ glands the eye muscle cells

the ear hormone secreting cells ~~the tongue~~ muscles light receptor cells

	Example	Make up part of...
Receptor	taste buds	the tongue
Effector		

The Nervous System

Q6 The diagram below shows a typical **neurone**.

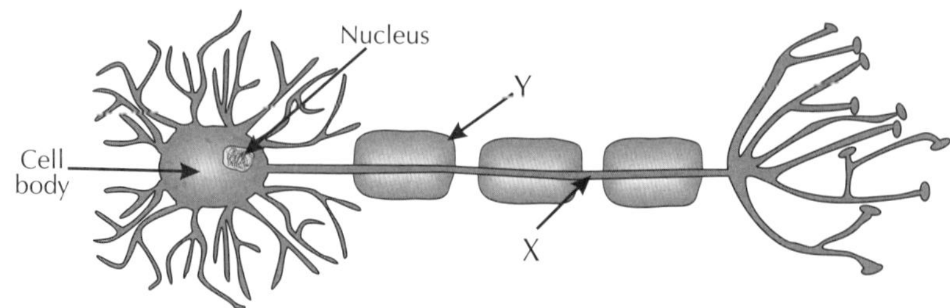

a) How does information travel along the neurone?

....

b) Complete the following sentences by circling the correct word in each pair.

> Structure X is the **synapse** / **axon** of the neurone. It's made from the neurone's **cytoplasm** / **nucleus** stretched into a long fibre and surrounded by a cell **membrane** / **wall**.

c) Name the part labelled **Y** and describe its function.

....

....

Q7 The neurones in the body **aren't directly connected** together — there are small **gaps** between them.

a) What **name** is given to the small gap between neurones?

....

b) Information is transmitted across the gap using **transmitter chemicals**. Explain how this works.

....

....

....

Q8 Some **drugs** affect **transmission** of impulses around the nervous system.

Describe an effect **ecstasy** (MDMA) has on the synapses in the brain and say why the drug is often described as having 'mood-enhancing effects'.

....

....

....

Reflexes

Q1 Circle the correct word(s) in each pair to complete the following sentences.

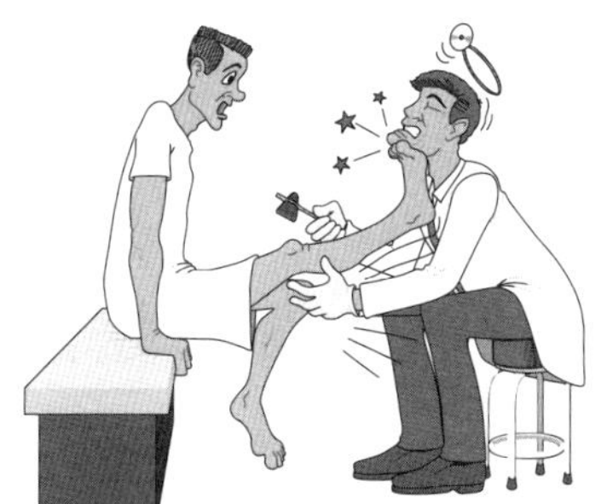

a) Reflexes happen more **quickly** / **slowly** than considered responses.

b) The neurones involved in reflexes go through the **back bone** / **spinal cord** or **an unconscious** / **a conscious** part of the brain.

c) Reflexes are **voluntary** / **involuntary**.

d) The main purpose of a reflex is to **protect** / **display** an organism.

e) The nervous pathway of a reflex is called a reflex **arc** / **ellipse**.

Q2 When you touch something **hot** with a finger you **automatically** pull the finger away. This is an example of a **reflex action**.

a) Complete the passage using words from the box below.

motor	sensory	receptors	effector	relay	stimulus	CNS

When the .... is detected by .... in the finger an impulse is sent along a .... neurone to the ....
The impulse is then passed to a .... neurone. The impulse is relayed to a .... neurone, which carries the impulse to the ....

b) The diagram opposite shows some parts of the nervous system involved in a reflex action.
Write the letter that shows:

i) a relay neurone ....

ii) a motor neurone ....

iii) a sensory neurone ....

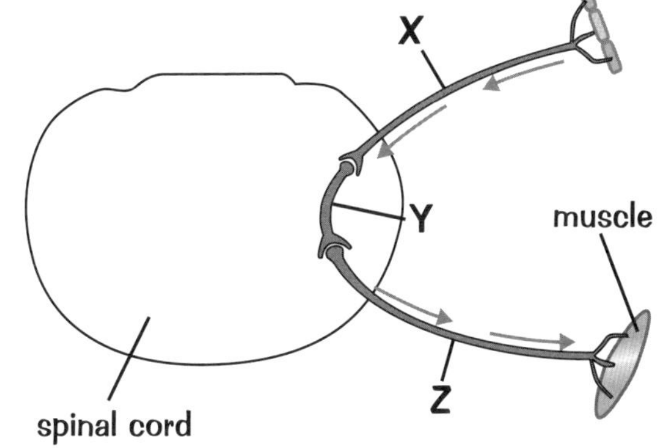

Top Tips: Reflexes are really fast — that's the whole point of them. And the fewer synapses the signals have to cross, the faster the reaction. Doctors test people's reflexes by tapping below their knees to make their legs jerk. This reflex takes less than 50 milliseconds as only two synapse are involved.

Reflexes

Q3 **Earthworms** rely on **reflexes** for most of their behaviour. Give one **disadvantage** of this.

....

....

Q4 Draw lines to match the reflex with the way in which it **helps** the animal **survive**.

a bird making its feathers stand on end

a turtle retracting its head and limbs into its shell

a jellyfish moving its tentacles when it senses movement

a spider running onto its web when it feels it move

a mollusc closing its shell

finding food

sheltering from a predator

finding a mate

Q5 Look carefully at the diagrams showing two different **eyes** below.

pupil

Eye A   Eye B

a) Which diagram do you think shows an eye in **bright light**? Give a reason for your answer.

....

....

b) Is the response illustrated by the diagrams above a **considered** response or a **reflex** response?

....

c) Why is it an **advantage** to have this type of response controlling the action of the eye?

....

....

....

Learning and Modifying Reflexes

Q1 Read the passage about **Ivan Pavlov** and answer the questions that follow.

> **Ivan Pavlov's most famous experiment looked at conditioning in dogs. The experiment was based on the observation that dogs salivated every time they smelt food. In his experiment a bell was rung just before the dogs were fed. Eventually he noticed that the dogs would salivate when the bell was rung even if they couldn't smell food.**

a) From the passage, identify the:

i) primary stimulus ....

ii) secondary stimulus ....

iii) unconditioned reflex ....

iv) conditioned reflex ....

b) Which reflex, conditioned or unconditioned, has been learnt?

....

c) Complete the following sentence by circling the correct words.

> In a conditioned reflex the final response has **a direct connection** / **no direct connection** to the secondary stimulus.

Q2 Birds can **learn** to reject insects with certain colourings — this is a **conditioned reflex**.

a) Put the following statements in order to show how a conditioned reflex can increase a bird's chances of survival. The first one has been done for you.

- [ ] **The bird spots a red coloured caterpillar and avoids it.**
- [ ] **The bird has increased its chances of survival by avoiding being poisoned.**
- [1] **A bird spots a red coloured caterpillar. It swoops down, catches and eats the caterpillar.**
- [ ] **The bird learns to associate feeling unwell with the bright colours.**
- [ ] **The bird feels unwell because of poisons in the insect.**

b) In this example, what is the **primary** stimulus?

....

Q3 Give one example of when it would be useful to **modify** a reflex response and describe in terms of neurones how the reflex arc is modified.

....

....

Brain Development and Learning

Q1 Tick the boxes to show whether each statement is **true** or **false**.

		True	False
a)	The brain contains around one million neurones.	☐	☐
b)	Complex animals with a brain are able to learn by experience.	☐	☐
c)	The brain coordinates complex behaviour such as social behaviour.	☐	☐

Q2 Complete the passage using words from the box below.

more experience unconnected less network
stimulated developed trillions formed

Most of the neurone connections in a newborn baby's brain are not yet ...., so the brain is only partly .... Every new .... causes the brain to become .... developed. When neurones in the brain are .... they branch out, forming connections between cells that were previously .... This forms a massive .... of neurones with .... of different routes for impulses to travel down.

Q3 Sarah and Sophie both play the **piano**. Sarah has been **practising** all week but Sophie **hasn't practised at all**. The girls' piano teacher, Mr Fudge, compliments Sarah on her performance but tells Sophie that he thinks she needs to practise more next week.

Explain why some skills can be **learnt** through **repetition**. Use diagrams to explain your answer.

....

....

....

....

....

Learning Skills and Behaviour

Q1 Explain why **complex animals**, such as humans, are able to **adapt** to new situations better than **simple animals**, such as insects.

....

....

Q2 Read the two case studies about **feral children** below and answer the questions that follow.

Isabelle was discovered in 1938 at the age of about six. She'd spent most of her life locked in a darkened room with her mother who was deaf and unable to speak. Isabelle was unable to walk and she had the mental age of a nineteen-month old child. She rapidly learnt to speak and write. By the age of eight Isabelle had reached a 'normal' level and was eventually able to go to school, participating in all activities with other children.

Eleven-year old Tissa was discovered in 1973 in Sri Lanka. When he was caught he showed many animal characteristics, such as walking on all fours, snarling at humans and yelping. Tissa was taken into care, and although he learned to smile and to eat with his hands, he never learned how to speak.

a) What is meant by the term '**critical period**'?

....

b) Do the case studies provide **evidence** of critical periods in child development? Explain your answer.

....

....

Q3 Hew has been in a **car accident**. Bruising on his **head** suggests that he took a nasty blow during the crash. The doctors are also concerned because he's having difficulty speaking and is unable to remember simple facts.

a) What part of Hew's **brain** might have been **damaged**?

....

b) Name **two** other things that this part of the brain is important for.

1. ....

2. ....

Top Tips: Language development isn't the only thing in humans with a critical period — binocular vision, balance and hearing do too. They don't just occur in humans either — e.g. some birds never learn the proper bird song for their species if they're kept in isolation when they're young.

Studying the Brain

Q1 Studying the brain can be useful for a number of reasons, for example in the **diagnosis** of people with brain disorders such as Parkinson's disease. Give **three methods** used by scientists to **map** the regions of the **cortex**.

1. ....

2. ....

3. ....

Q2 There are two main types of **memory** — **short-term** and **long-term**.

a) Where are the following memories likely to be stored? Put a letter **S** in the boxes next to any memories likely to be stored in **short-term** memory and a letter **L** in those likely to be stored in **long-term** memory.

The rides you went on when you visited a theme park last month. ☐

The smell of hot apple pie drifting through from the kitchen as it's being baked. ☐

What you had for tea last Wednesday. ☐

Something that happened in an episode of The Bill half an hour ago. ☐

What your great aunt Gladys got you for your birthday when you were fourteen. ☐

Answering a question in an exam about a topic you learnt two months ago. ☐

b) There are a number of things that can influence how humans remember information.

i) Jerry is trying to remember two phone numbers:

A. 01951 845217 and B. 01234 543210

Which number, A or B, is Jerry most likely to remember? Give a reason for your answer.

....

....

ii) If **strong stimuli** are associated with information it can help people remember more. Give **three** of these stimuli.

1. .... 2. .... 3. ....

iii) Give **one** other method used by humans to make them **more likely** to remember information.

....

Memory Mapping

Q1 Read the passage below and answer the questions that follow.

The ability to store information in our brains, for retrieval later on, is something that most of us take for granted. However, the mechanisms that underlie memory are not yet fully understood. What is known is that certain areas of the brain are crucial for memory processing. The discovery of some of these areas has come from attempts to treat people with epilepsy.

Epilepsy is a condition that causes sufferers to have repeated seizures. The cause of a seizure is not usually known, but they are always accompanied by a change in the electrical activity in the cerebral cortex of the brain. The abnormal electrical activity tends to start in an area where the neurones are highly sensitive, and then spread out across the cortex. Epileptic seizures can often be controlled using anticonvulsant drugs, and sometimes with surgery.

Between the 1930s and 1950s, Wilder Penfield investigated the areas of his patients' brains that were prone to seizures using electrical stimulation. By systematically stimulating points in the cortex, Penfield was able to determine the link between certain areas and their functions. For example, when he stimulated a particular area patients would feel tingling sensations in their skin, showing that this area was involved in the sense of touch. When he stimulated a region of the brain called the temporal lobe (shown in the diagram) some of his patients seemed to experience memories of past events — suggesting that the temporal lobe is part of the system for recalling stored memories.

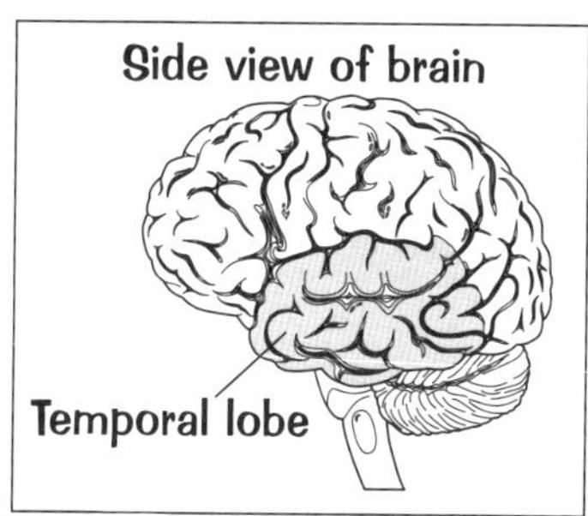

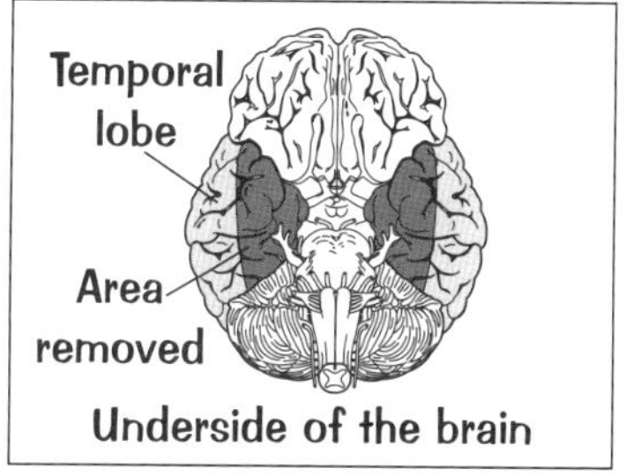

Further evidence for the involvement of the temporal lobe in memory came from a patient who was given surgery for his epilepsy in 1953. The patient, known as H.M., had part of the temporal lobe on both sides of his brain removed to try to control his seizures. The diagram shows the areas removed. The operation was successful, in that H.M.'s seizures were reduced, but it left him with severe amnesia (memory loss). The interesting thing about H.M.'s amnesia was that it was very selective. H.M. can remember the experiences of his childhood, showing that his long-term memories stored before the operation were not affected. He is also able to learn new tasks and retain details of what he is doing, showing that his short-term memory still works. However, what H.M. can't do is form any new long-term memories. For example, the doctor who has worked with H.M. for over 40 years since the operation has to reintroduce herself every time they meet — H.M. has no memory of who she is.

Since the case of H.M. doctors have investigated other ways to map the areas of a patient's brain involved in memory. One method currently used is to take MRI scans of a patient's brain while they are performing memory tasks. MRI scans use a strong magnetic field to monitor changes in the blood flow around the brain and highlight areas of high activity. The theory is that by working out the areas that are active during the memory tasks, the scientist can determine which areas are needed for memory processing.

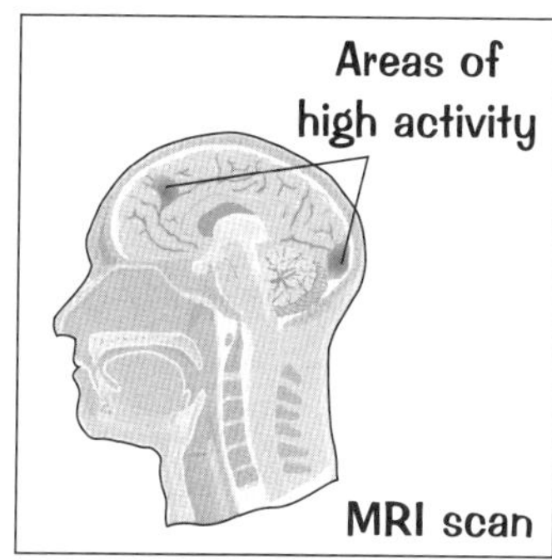

It is hoped that in the future a model will be devised that fully explains how our brains process memories — until then it remains an ongoing area of research.

Memory Mapping

a) Complete the definition of memory by filling in the blanks.

Memory is the .... and .... of information.

b) Briefly describe how each of the methods described in the article was useful in determining the areas of the brain associated with memory:

i) Electrical stimulation. ....

....

ii) Study of H.M. ....

....

iii) MRI scans during memory tasks. ....

....

c) What **type** of memory was recalled when Penfield stimulated the temporal lobe? Circle the correct answer.

long-term memory   short-term memory   mid-term memory

d) Why was the patient H.M. so useful in determining the function of certain brain areas?

....

e) Describe which parts of H.M.'s memory were:

i) **Unaffected** by his operation.

....

....

ii) **Damaged** by his operation.

....

....

f) Why is the study of memory an ongoing area of research?

....

....

....

H.M.'s memory is an ongoing area of research, and an important tourist attraction.

Industrial Chemical Synthesis

Q1 Explain what is meant by **chemical synthesis**.

....

Q2 Tick the boxes to show whether the following are usually produced on a **small** or **large scale**.

		Small scale	Large scale
a)	Pharmaceuticals	☐	☐
b)	Sulfuric acid	☐	☐
c)	Fertiliser	☐	☐

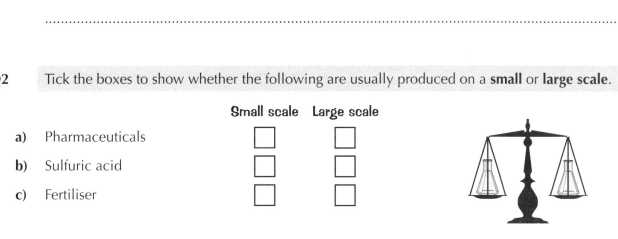

Q3 Modern industry uses thousands of tonnes of **sulfuric acid** per day. The pie chart shows the major **uses** of the sulfuric acid produced by a particular plant.

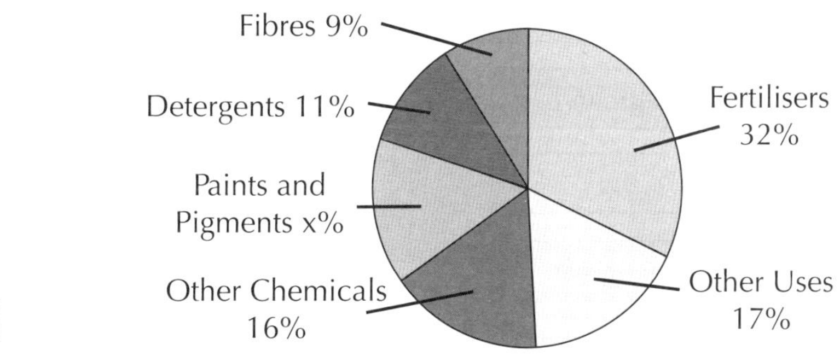

a) What is the **main use** of the sulfuric acid from this plant?

....

b) What percentage of the sulfuric acid from this plant is used in the production of paints and pigments?

....

Q4 The bar chart shows the number of people **employed** in various sectors of the **chemical industry** in country X.

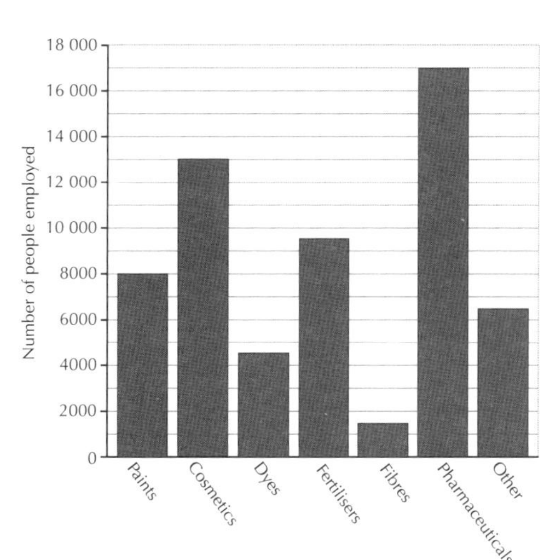

a) Which **sector** employs the **most** people?

....

b) How many people **in total** are employed in the chemical industry in country X?

....

Acids and Alkalis

Q1 Complete each of the following sentences with a single word.

a) Solutions which are not acidic or alkaline are said to be ....

b) A neutral substance has a pH of ....

c) Universal indicator is a combination of different ....

d) An alkali is a substance with a pH of .... than 7.

Q2 Draw lines to match the substances and their universal indicator colours to their **pH** values and **acid/alkali strengths**.

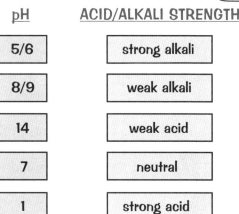

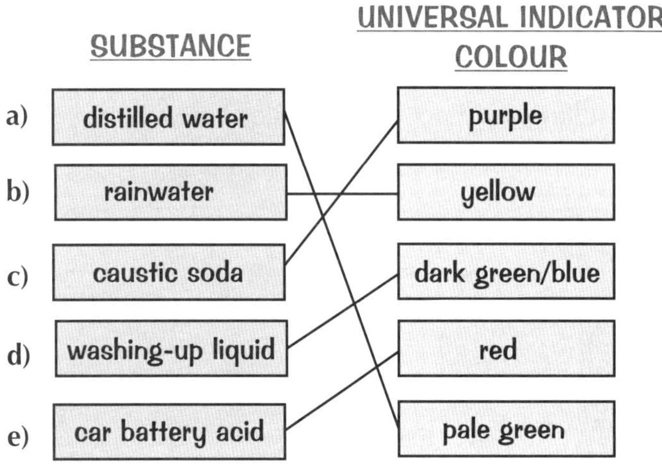

pH	ACID/ALKALI STRENGTH
5/6	strong alkali
8/9	weak alkali
14	weak acid
7	neutral
1	strong acid

Q3 Many chemicals that people use **every day** are **acids** or **alkalis**.

a) Complete the following passage using words from the box.

hydrogen chloride	solids	more	tartaric	ethanoic	less	liquid	nitric

Acids are substances with a pH of .... than 7.
Pure acidic compounds are found in various different states, for example citric acid and .... acid are both ....
Sulfuric acid is an example of a .... acidic compound, as are .... and .... acids.
There are also acidic compounds that are gases — .... is one example.

b) Name three common **alkalis** that are **hydroxides**.

....

Acids and Alkalis

Q4 **Indigestion** is caused by **too much acid** in the stomach.
Antacid tablets contain **alkalis**, which neutralise the excess acid.

a) Which is the correct word equation for a **neutralisation reaction**? Circle the correct answer.

salt + acid → alkali + water   acid + alkali → salt + water   acid + water → alkali + salt

b) Say what is produced when:

i) an acidic compound is dissolved in water.

....

ii) an alkaline compound is dissolved in water.

....

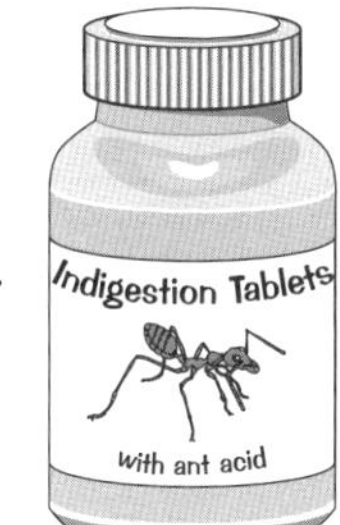

Joey wanted to test whether some antacid tablets really did **neutralise acid**. He added a tablet to some hydrochloric acid, stirred it until it dissolved and tested the pH of the solution. Further tests were carried out after dissolving a second, third and fourth tablet.
His results are shown in the table below.

Tablets added	pH of acid
0	1
1	2
2	3
3	7
4	7

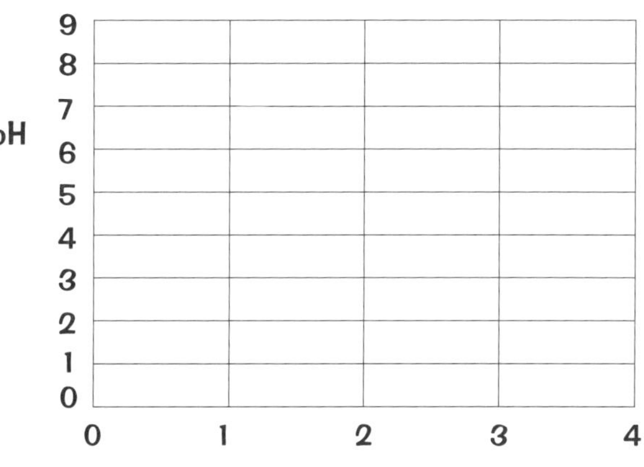

c) **i)** Plot a graph of the results on the grid shown.

ii) How many tablets were needed to neutralise the acid? ....

d) Give two ways Joey could have tested the pH of the solution.

1. ....

2. ....

Q5 When an acid and an alkali react the products are **neutral**. This is called a **neutralisation** reaction.

a) Describe what happens to the **hydrogen ions** from the acid and the **hydroxide ions** from the alkali during a neutralisation reaction.

....

b) Write a balanced symbol equation to illustrate the reaction between the **hydrogen ions** from the acid and the **hydroxide ions** from the alkali during a neutralisation reaction.

....

Acids Reacting with Metals

Q1 The diagram below shows **magnesium** reacting with **hydrochloric acid**.

a) Label the diagram with the names of the chemicals.

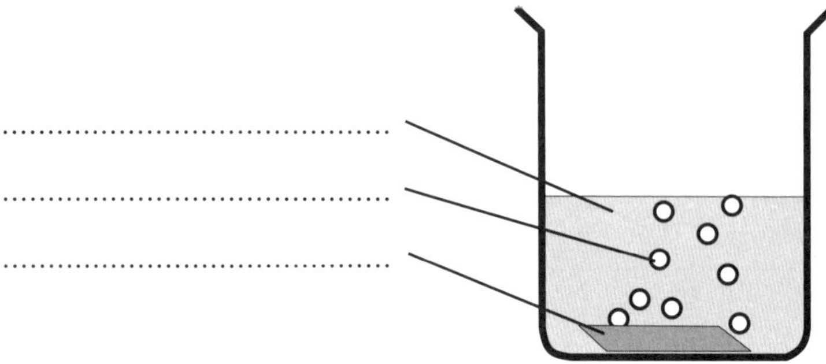

b) Complete the word equation for this reaction:

magnesium + ... → **magnesium chloride +** ....

c) Write a **balanced** symbol equation for the reaction.

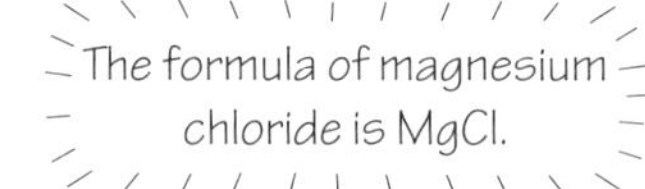
The formula of magnesium
chloride is MgCl.

....

d) All metals will react with acids in a similar way.
Zinc reacts with sulfuric acid. Give the **word** equation for this reaction.

....

Q2 Write out **balanced** symbol equations for the following reactions. Include **state symbols**.

a) calcium + hydrochloric acid

....

b) zinc + hydrochloric acid

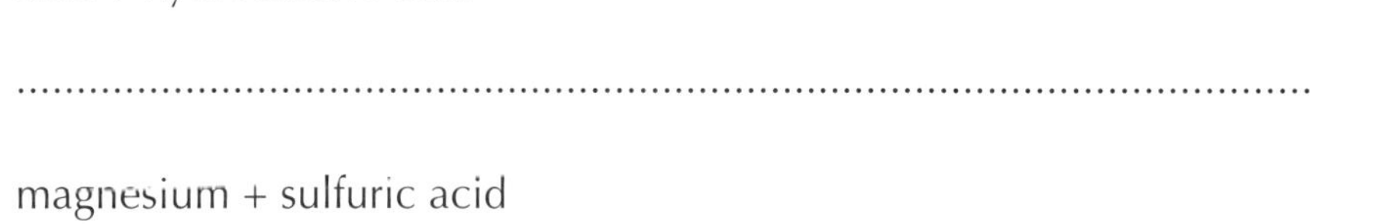

....

c) magnesium + sulfuric acid

....

d) **Hydrobromic acid** reacts with **magnesium** to form a bromide salt and hydrogen, as shown in the equation below.

$$Mg(s) + 2HBr(l) \rightarrow MgBr_2(aq) + H_2(g)$$

Write a balanced symbol equation for the reaction between **aluminium** and hydrobromic acid. (The formula of aluminium bromide is $AlBr_3$.)

....

Oxides, Hydroxides and Carbonates

Q1 Give the **general word equation** for the reaction between an **acid** and:

a) a metal oxide ....

b) a metal carbonate ....

c) a metal hydroxide ....

Q2 Fill in the blanks to complete the word equations for **acids** reacting with **metal oxides** and **metal hydroxides**.

A metal-ox-hide

a) hydrochloric acid + lead oxide → .... chloride + water

b) nitric acid + copper hydroxide → copper .... + water

c) sulfuric acid + zinc oxide → zinc sulfate + ...

d) hydrochloric acid + ... oxide → nickel .... + ...

e) .... acid + copper oxide → .... nitrate + ...

f) sulfuric acid + ... hydroxide → sodium .... + ...

Q3 Complete the following symbol equations for **acids** reacting with **metal carbonates**.

a) $2HNO_3(l) + Na_2CO_3(s) \rightarrow$ .... + ... + ...

b) $H_2SO_4(l) +$ .... $\rightarrow MgSO_4(aq) +$ .... + ...

Q4 Write symbol equations for the following reactions.

a) sulfuric acid + copper oxide

....

The formula of copper oxide is CuO.

b) nitric acid + magnesium oxide

....

c) sulfuric acid + sodium hydroxide

....

Top Tips: At first glance it looks quite scary, all this writing equations — but it's not that bad, honest. The key is to learn the basic rules inside out. Once you've got them mastered it's really just a case of swapping a few bits round and filling in the gaps. No reason to panic at all.

Oxides, Hydroxides and Carbonates

Q5 **Acids** react with **metal carbonates** in neutralisation reactions. Write **balanced symbol equations** for the following reactions.

a) hydrochloric acid + copper carbonate

....

The formula of copper carbonate is $CuCO_3$.

b) nitric acid + magnesium carbonate

....

c) sulfuric acid + lithium carbonate

....

The formula of lithium carbonate is $LiCO_3$.

d) hydrochloric acid + calcium carbonate

....

e) sulfuric acid + sodium carbonate

....

Q6 Amir was investigating how he could restore a tarnished copper ornament. He obtained some **copper compounds** and looked at the effect of reacting them with dilute **hydrochloric acid** (HCl).

SUBSTANCE TESTED	FORMULA	COLOUR	OBSERVATIONS WHEN ADDED TO THE ACID
copper carbonate	$CuCO_3$	green	fizzed and dissolved forming a blue solution
copper hydroxide	$Cu(OH)_2$	blue	dissolved slowly forming a blue solution
copper oxide	CuO	black	dissolved very slowly forming a blue solution

a) **i)** Why does copper carbonate fizz when it reacts with an acid?

....

ii) Write a word equation for the reaction between hydrochloric acid and copper carbonate.

....

b) Amir tested part of the copper ornament with the acid and it fizzed. Which compound is likely to be present on the surface of the ornament?

....

No.1 Copper

c) Write a balanced symbol equation for the reaction of hydrochloric acid with copper hydroxide.

....

Synthesising Compounds

Q1 Draw lines to match each description to the type of reaction it is describing.

an acid and an alkali react to produce a salt	precipitation
a compound breaks down on heating	neutralisation
an insoluble solid forms when two solutions are mixed	thermal decomposition

Q2 In the synthesis of any **organic chemical** there are a number of **important stages**.

a) Complete the passage using words from the box below.

harmed	reduce	hazards	injury	action

A risk assessment should identify any stage in the process that could cause .... This usually involves identifying .... and the people who might be .... Risk assessments also include what .... can be taken to .... the risk.

b) When making a chemical on an industrial scale it is often important to calculate accurately the quantities of reactants to be used. Explain why.

....

....

c) Give **two** factors that should be considered when choosing the apparatus in which a reaction will be carried out.

....

....

Q3 Explain why each of the following might be carried out during chemical synthesis.

a) Filtration

....

b) Evaporation

....

c) Drying

....

Synthesising Compounds

Q4 Read the article below and answer the questions that follow.

Sodium Bromide

To most people sodium bromide looks like any other white, crystalline salt. What people don't realise is the vast number of uses it has in the chemical industry, ranging from photography to pharmaceuticals. As with most inorganic chemicals, there are a number of different stages in the production of sodium bromide.

Industrial Synthesis

Sodium bromide (NaBr) is usually produced by reacting sodium hydroxide (NaOH) with hydrobromic acid (HBr):

Sodium hydroxide + hydrobromic acid → sodium bromide + water

Although this is a relatively simple reaction, the plant used to produce sodium bromide is quite high-tech. Sodium hydroxide is highly reactive so it's important to use the right equipment. The reaction vessel must be able to withstand the corrosive effects of sodium hydroxide and the large amount of heat produced when it reacts with hydrobromic acid.

The production of sodium bromide doesn't involve a catalyst, so the main way to control the rate of reaction is to alter the concentrations of the reactants.

After reacting sodium hydroxide with hydrobromic acid, the sodium bromide is extracted by evaporation — this involves heating the sodium bromide solution. The water is evaporated, leaving behind white crystals of sodium bromide. After the product has been isolated it is then purified.

Yield and purity

The yield of sodium bromide produced is then calculated. For financial reasons it's important to produce a high yield, so chemical engineers are always looking for ways to modify the process to give a higher yield. The purity of the product is also calculated at this stage.

Safety

People working on sodium bromide production need to take a number of safety precautions. This is because of the highly corrosive and reactive nature of the sodium hydroxide. Sodium bromide also has its risks — it's harmful if swallowed and can irritate the skin and eyes.

Uses of sodium bromide

Sodium bromide has a range of different uses in the chemical industry. The data on the right is from a large chemical company that supplies sodium bromide to different sectors in the chemical industry. It shows what the sodium bromide it produces is used for.

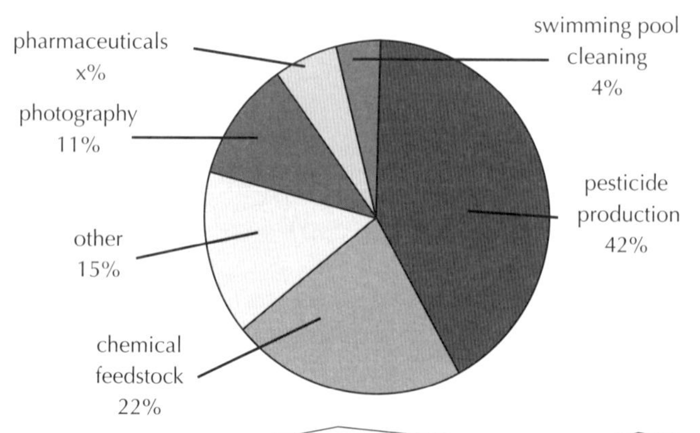

Synthesising Compounds

a) i) What **type** of reaction is used to produce sodium bromide?

....

ii) Write a balanced symbol equation (including state symbols) to show the formation of sodium bromide.

....

b) Give **two** reasons why it is important to choose a suitable reaction vessel for the production of sodium bromide.

....

....

c) Suggest why **evaporation** is used to separate the sodium bromide from the reaction mixture.

....

d) Suggest a method that could be used to **purify** the sodium bromide.

....

e) The article describes how sodium hydroxide and sodium bromide are dangerous.

i) When planning the synthesis of any compound, what is the process of identifying possible hazards called?

....

ii) Give two hazards associated with **sodium bromide**.

....

....

f) Why is it useful to calculate the **yield** of sodium bromide?

....

g) i) Which industry does the company in the article supply the most sodium bromide to?

....

ii) What percentage of their sodium bromide is used in the pharmaceutical industry?

....

iii) If the company produces 3000 tonnes of sodium bromide per year, what **mass** is used in photography?

....

Relative Formula Mass

Q1 All elements have a relative atomic mass, A_r.

a) Complete the following sentence by filling in the blanks.

> The relative atomic mass of an element shows the .... of its atoms relative to the mass of one .... of ....

b) Give the **relative atomic masses** (A_r) of the following elements. Use the periodic table to help you.

i) magnesium ....
ii) neon ....
iii) oxygen ....
iv) hydrogen ....
v) C ....
vi) Cu ....
vii) K ....
viii) Ca ....
ix) Cl ....

Q2 Use the periodic table to identify the elements A, B and C.

> Element A has an A_r of 4.
> Element B has an A_r 3 times that of element A.
> Element C has an A_r 4 times that of element A.

Element A = ...

Element B = ...

Element C = ...

A_r me hearties

Q3 a) Explain how the **relative formula mass** of a **compound** is calculated.

....

b) Give the **relative formula masses** (M_r) of the following:

i) water, H_2O ....

ii) potassium chloride, KOH ....

iii) nitric acid, HNO_3 ....

iv) magnesium hydroxide, $Mg(OH)_2$ ....

v) iron(III) hydroxide, $Fe(OH)_3$ ....

Top Tips: The periodic table really comes in useful here. There's no way you'll be able to answer these questions without one (unless you've memorised all the elements' relative atomic masses — and that would just be silly). And luckily for you, you'll be given one in your exam. Yay!

Calculating Masses in Reactions

Q1 Anna burns **10 g** of **magnesium** in air to produce **magnesium oxide** (MgO).

a) Write out the **balanced equation** for this reaction.

....

b) Calculate the mass of **magnesium oxide** that's produced.

....

....

....

magnesium + oxygen

Q2 What mass of **sodium** is needed to make **2 g** of **sodium oxide**?

$$4Na + O_2 \rightarrow 2Na_2O$$

....

....

....

Q3 **Aluminium** and **iron oxide** (Fe_2O_3) react together to produce **aluminium oxide** (Al_2O_3) and **iron**.

a) Write out the **balanced equation** for this reaction.

....

b) What **mass** of iron is produced from **20 g** of iron oxide?

....

....

....

Q4 When heated, **limestone** ($CaCO_3$) decomposes to form **calcium oxide** (CaO) and **carbon dioxide**.

How many **kilograms** of limestone are needed to make **100 kilograms** of **calcium oxide**?

The calculation is exactly the same — just use 'kg' instead of 'g'.

....

....

....

....

Calculating Masses in Reactions

Q5 **Iron oxide** is reduced to **iron** inside a blast furnace using carbon. There are **three** stages involved.

Stage A	$C + O_2 \rightarrow CO_2$
Stage B	$CO_2 + C \rightarrow 2CO$
Stage C	$3CO + Fe_2O_3 \rightarrow 2Fe + 3CO_2$

If **10 g** of **carbon** are used in stage B, and all the carbon monoxide produced gets used in stage C, what **mass** of $\mathbf{CO_2}$ is produced in **stage C**?

....

....

....

....

Work out the mass of CO at the end of stage B first.

Q6 **Sodium sulfate** (Na_2SO_4) is made by reacting **sodium hydroxide** (NaOH) with **sulfuric acid** (H_2SO_4). **Water** is also produced.

a) Write out the **balanced equation** for this reaction.

....

b) What mass of **sodium hydroxide** is needed to make **75 g** of **sodium sulfate**?

....

....

....

....

c) What mass of **water** is formed when **50 g** of **sulfuric acid** reacts?

....

....

....

....

Isolating the Product and Measuring Yield

Q1 James wanted to produce **silver chloride** (AgCl). He added a carefully measured mass of silver nitrate to some dilute hydrochloric acid. An **insoluble white solid** formed.

a) Complete the formula for calculating percentage yield, and its labels, using words from the box. Words can be used more than once.

reactants	weighing	theoretical yield	pure	dried	actual yield	maximum

This is the mass of pure dry product. It is found by .... the dried product.

percentage yield = $\dfrac{\text{..}}{\text{..}}$ × 100

This is the .... of the product as a percentage of the ....

This is the .... amount of ...., dried product that could have been made using the amounts of .... you started with.

b) James calculated that he should get 2.7 g of silver chloride, but he only got 1.2 g. What was the **percentage yield**?

....

c) What **method** should James use to separate silver chloride from the solution?

....

Silver chloride is an insoluble solid.

d) James left the silver chloride to dry on the bench. Suggest two ways the product could have been dried if the reaction was being carried out on a large scale.

1. ....

2. ....

Q2 Emilio and Julio need to separate a **soluble solid** from a **solution**.

a) Suggest a method they could use to separate the soluble solid from solution.

....

b) How can the method you suggested in part a) be useful when purifying a product?

....

Titrations

Q1 **Titrations** are used widely in industry, for example when determining the **purity** of a substance.

a) If a solid product is being tested why must it first be made into a **solution**?

....

b) Fill in the blanks using words from the box below to describe how a solution is made and draw lines to connect each statement to the diagram it describes. You can use the words more than once.

solvent	weigh	swirl	dissolved	crush	water	titration

① .... the solid product into a powder.

② .... some of the powdered product into a .... flask.

③ The powder is then .... by adding some .... (e.g. ....).

④ .... the flask until all of the solid has ....

c) Label the following pieces of apparatus used in a titration experiment.

....

....

d) Describe how you would carry out a titration.

....

....

....

Talk about tight rations.

Purity

Q1 **Pharmaceutical companies** need to ensure that the drugs they produce are **pure**.

a) Give two methods that can be used to improve the purity of a product.

1. .... 2. ....

b) Why is it important to control the purity of chemicals such as pharmaceuticals?

....

....

Q2 Ruth works in the quality assurance department of a company that produces **fizzy drinks**. The drinks contain **citric acid**. One of Ruth's jobs is to test the **purity** of the citric acid before it is used to make the drinks. She does this by carrying out an acid-alkali **titration**.

a) What type of reaction do titrations involve? Circle the correct answer.

precipitation esterification neutralisation

b) Ruth starts off with **0.3 g of citric acid** dissolved in **25 cm³** of water. When she carries out the titration she finds that it takes **21.6 cm³ of 2.5 g/dm³ sodium hydroxide** (NaOH) to neutralise the citric acid. Calculate the purity of the citric acid by completing the following steps.

i) Calculate the **concentration** of the citric acid solution using the equation:

$$\text{conc. of citric acid solution} = 4.8 \times \frac{\text{conc. of NaOH} \times \text{vol. of NaOH}}{\text{vol. of citric acid solution}}$$

....

....

ii) Calculate the **mass** of the citric acid using the equation:

$$\text{mass of citric acid} = \text{concentration of citric acid} \times \text{volume}$$

....

iii) Calculate the **percentage purity** of the citric acid using the equation:

$$\text{\% purity} = \frac{\text{calculated mass of citric acid}}{\text{mass of citric acid at start}} \times 100\%$$

....

....

Rates of Reaction

Q1 a) Match these common chemical reactions to the **speed** at which they happen.

a firework exploding

hair being dyed

an apple rotting

SLOW (hours or longer)

MODERATE SPEED (minutes)

FAST (seconds or shorter)

a match burning

a ship rusting

b) Explain what is meant by the term 'rate of chemical reaction'.

....

....

Q2 When chemicals are produced on an **industrial scale** it is important to control the **rates of reactions**.

Complete the passage below using words from the box.

explosion	economic	costs	fast	safety	optimum	yield	compromise

The rates of reactions in industrial chemical synthesis need to be controlled for two main reasons. Firstly for .... reasons. If the reaction is too .... it could cause an ...., which may injure or even kill employees. Chemical reactions are also controlled for .... reasons. Companies usually choose .... conditions. These will usually involve a .... between the ...., rate of reaction and production ....

Q3 The graph shows the results from an experiment using **magnesium** and dilute **hydrochloric acid**. The **volume of gas** produced was measured at regular intervals as the reaction proceeded.

Volume of gas produced

R

Q

P

Time (s)

a) Which reaction was **faster**, P or Q?

....

b) Which reaction produced the **largest volume of gas**, P, Q or R?

....

c) On the curve for reaction R, mark with an **X** the point where the reaction finishes.

Rates of Reaction

Q4 Circle the correct words to complete the sentences below.

a) The **higher** / **lower** the temperature, the faster the rate of reaction.

b) A **higher** / **lower** concentration will reduce the rate of reaction.

c) A smaller particle size **increases** / **decreases** the rate of reaction.

d) Using a catalyst **increases** / **decreases** the rate of reaction.

Nora's reactions were slow in the cold.

Q5 In an experiment to investigate **reaction rates**, strips of **magnesium** were put into tubes containing different concentrations of **hydrochloric acid**. The time taken for the magnesium to 'disappear' was measured. The results are shown in the table.

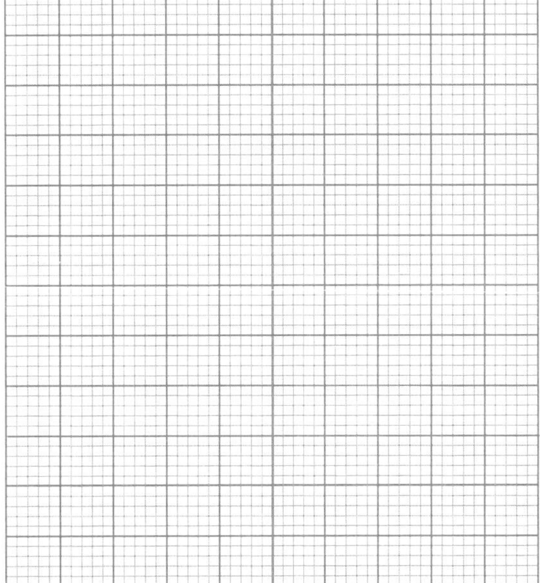

Conc. of acid (mol/dm^3)	Time taken (seconds)
0.01	298
0.02	147
0.04	74
0.08	37
0.10	30
0.20	15

a) Give **three** things that should be kept the same in each case to make this a **fair test**.

....

....

b) Plot a graph of the data on the grid provided, with concentration of acid on the horizontal axis and time on the vertical axis.

c) What do the results tell you about how the concentration of acid affects the rate of the reaction?

....

d) Would the rates of the reaction have been different if magnesium powder had been used instead? If so, how?

....

....

Top Tips: It's a pretty good idea to learn the four things that reaction rate depends on (temperature, concentration, surface area and using a catalyst). It's an even better idea to learn exactly how these four things affect the rate of a reaction and what happens when you change them.

Collision Theory

Q1 Complete the following passage by circling the correct word(s) from each pair.

In order for a reaction to occur, the particles must **remain still** / **collide**. If you heat up a reaction mixture, you give the particles more **energy** / **surface area**. This makes them move **faster** / **more slowly** and so there is **more** / **less** chance of successful collisions. So, increasing the temperature increases the **concentration** / **rate of reaction**.

Q2 Reactions involving solutions are affected by the **concentration**.

a) If you increase the concentration of a solution, does the rate of reaction **increase** or **decrease**? Explain your answer.

....

....

b) In the boxes on the right, draw two diagrams, one showing a solution containing two different types of particle at low concentration, the other showing a high concentration of the solution.

low concentration | high concentration

Q3 Here are five statements about **surface area** and rates of reaction. Tick the appropriate box to show whether each is **true** or **false**.

		True	False
a)	Breaking a solid into smaller pieces decreases its surface area.	☐	☐
b)	A larger surface area will mean a faster rate of reaction.	☐	☐
c)	A larger surface area decreases the number of useful collisions.	☐	☐
d)	Powdered marble has a larger surface area than the same mass of marble chips.	☐	☐
e)	A powdered solid reactant produces more product overall than an equal mass of reactant in large lumps does.	☐	☐

Q4 Some reactions use **catalysts**. What is a catalyst?

....

....

Measuring Rates of Reaction

Q1 Complete the following sentence by circling the correct word from each pair.

The **speed** / **volume** of a reaction can be measured by observing either how quickly the **products** / **reactants** are used up or how quickly the **products** / **reactants** are formed.

Q2 Charlie was comparing the rate of reaction of 5 g of magnesium ribbon with 20 ml of **five different concentrations** of hydrochloric acid. Each time he measured the volume of **gas** that was produced during the **first minute** of the reaction.

a) In the space below draw the apparatus that Charlie could use to measure the **volume** of gas produced.

b) Describe what Charlie could do if he wanted to follow the rate of reaction by calculating the change in **mass** over the course of the reaction.

....

....

....

Q3 Horatio was investigating the reaction between **lead nitrate** and different concentrations of **hydrochloric acid**. When lead nitrate and hydrochloric acid react they produce **lead chloride**, which is an **insoluble solid**.

a) What name is given to this type of reaction?

....

acid concentration

b) Describe how Horatio could measure the rate of reaction.

....

....

....

Waves — The Basics

Q1 Complete the sentence below by circling the correct word in each pair.

Waves transfer energy / matter without transferring any energy / matter.

Q2 All waves have a **frequency** and a **wavelength**.

a) What units are used to measure wavelength? ....

b) What does it mean to say that "the frequency of a wave is 25 hertz"?

....

c) The diagram shows a waveform.
Which of A, B or C is the length of one whole wave?

....

A
B
C

Q3 There are **two ways** in which you can make waves on a **slinky** spring.

a) Which diagram shows a **transverse** wave, and which one shows a **longitudinal** wave?

Transverse: ....

Longitudinal: ....

1 2

b) Write down one difference between these two types of wave.

....

Q4 Jason draws the graph below to show a wave with an **amplitude** of **4 m** and a **wavelength** of **2 m**.

a) What has Jason done wrong?

....

....

b) On the same set of axes, draw a wave with a **wavelength** of **5 m** and an **amplitude** of **3 m**.

m 4 2 0 -2 -4
2 4 6 8 m

Q5 **Green light** travels at 3×10^8 m/s and has a wavelength of about 5×10^{-7} m.

Calculate the **frequency** of green light. Give the correct unit in your answer.

....

....

Wave Properties

Q1 Harriet spends at least an hour looking at herself in a **mirror** every day. The image she sees is formed from light reflected by the mirror.

a) What is meant by a "normal" when talking about reflection?

....

....

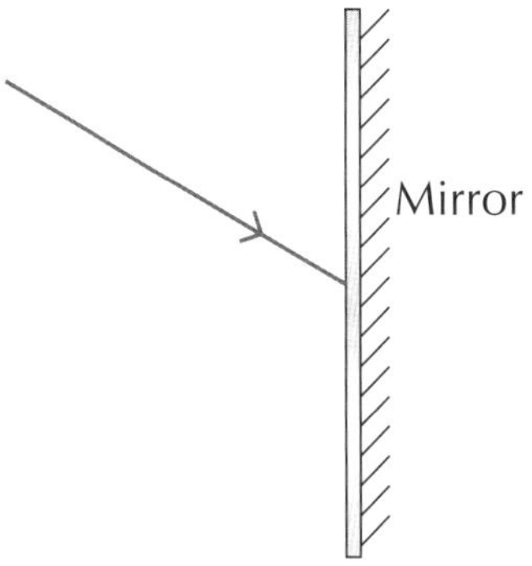

b) Complete the diagram to show an incident ray of light being reflected by the mirror. Label the **angle of incidence** ,**i**, the **normal**, and the **angle of reflection**, **r**.

Mirror

Q2 When a wave passes into a different substance, it may change **speed**.

Cross out words in the statements below to make them correct.

a) When a wave **slows down**, it may bend **towards** / **away from** the normal. The wavelength **gets longer** / **gets shorter** / **stays the same**. The frequency **increases** / **decreases** / **stays the same**.

b) When a wave **speeds up**, it may bend **towards** / **away from** the normal. The wavelength **gets longer** / **gets shorter** / **stays the same**. The frequency **increases** / **decreases** / **stays the same**.

Q3 The diagram shows a light ray passing through **air** and through **glass**.

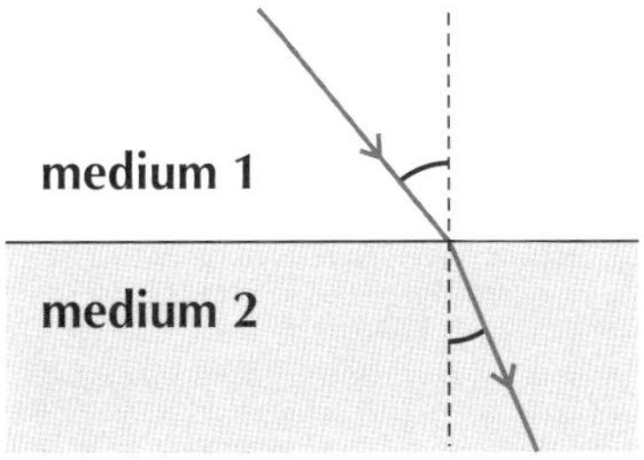

medium 1

medium 2

Remember glass is denser than air.

D

a) Fill in the gaps in this sentence to say which medium is **air** and which is **glass**.

Medium 1 in the diagram is .... and **medium 2** is ....

b) **Explain** your answer to part a).

....

c) Would your answer to a) be the **same** if the wave was a **sound wave**? Explain why.

....

Wave Properties

Q4 Diagrams A and B show plane **water waves** travelling from **deep** to **shallow** water in a ripple tank.

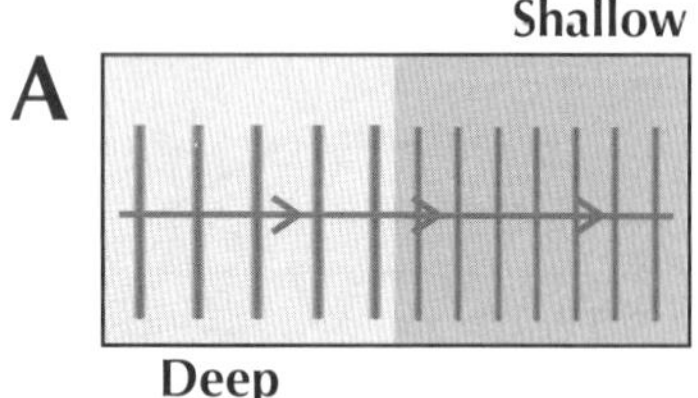

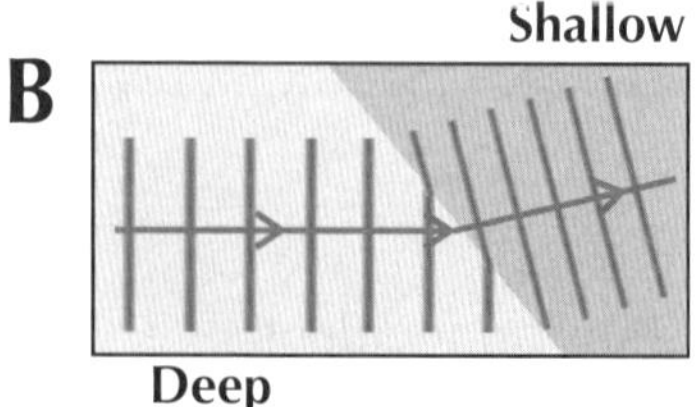

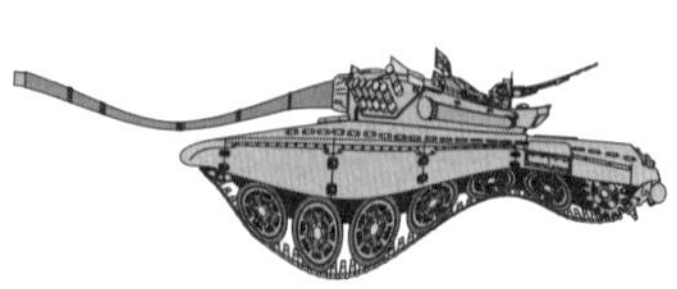

a) Which diagram shows the waves being **refracted**? ....

b) Why does refraction **not happen** in the other diagram?

....

c) What happens to the **wavelength** of the waves as they pass into shallower water?

....

d) What happens to the **frequency** of the waves as they pass into the shallower water?

....

e) What happens to the **velocity** of the waves as they pass into the shallower water?

....

f) Imagine that the wave in the shallow water in diagram B passes into **deeper water** again. What would you expect to happen to the wave?

Think about wavelength, frequency and speed.

....

....

Q5 Emma is doing her homework, which is about **total internal reflection**.

a) What is meant by total internal reflection?

....

....

b) In which of these situations could you get total internal reflection? Circle the correct letter(s).

A Light is coming out of air into water.
B Light is coming out of glass into air.

Wave Properties

Q6 Explain what is meant by the '**critical angle**' for a boundary between two materials.

....

....

Q7 The critical angle for glass/air is 42°.

Complete the ray diagrams below.

You'll need to measure the angle of incidence for each one — carefully.

Critical angle at toe/banana boundary: 87°

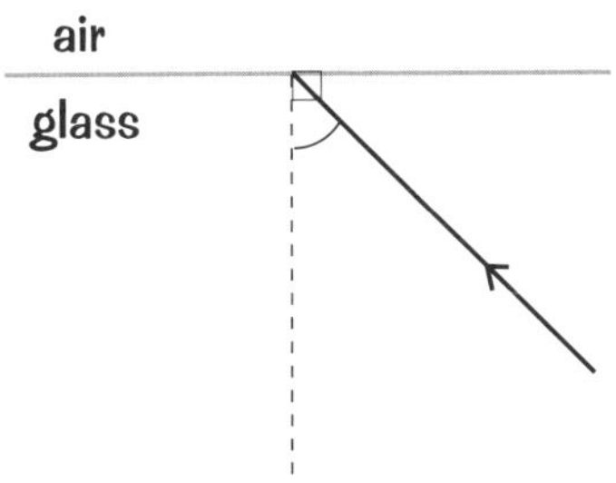

air
glass

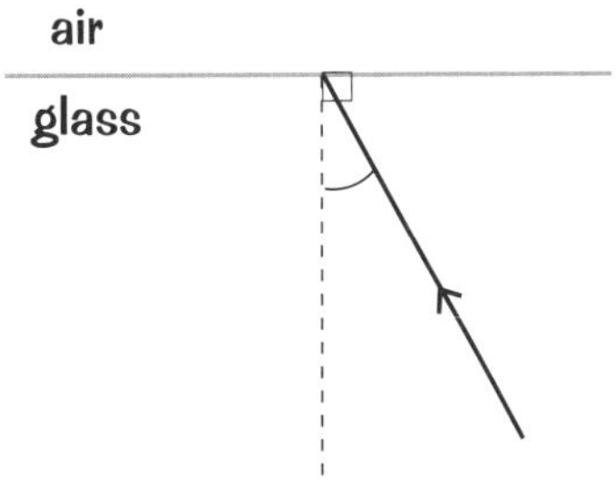

air
glass

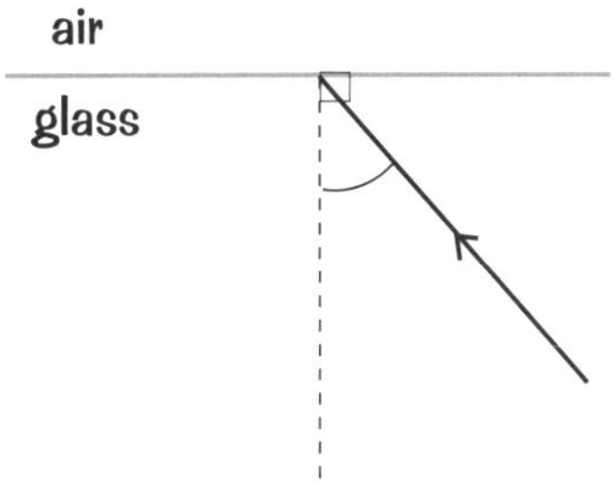

air
glass

Q8 Another important property of waves is **diffraction**.

a) Explain what 'diffraction' means.

....

....

b) A ripple tank is used to study the behaviour of waves as they pass through gaps. The gap in diagram 1 is about the **same size** as the wavelength. The gap in diagram 2 is **much bigger**. Complete both diagrams to show what happens to the waves after they pass through the gaps.

(1)

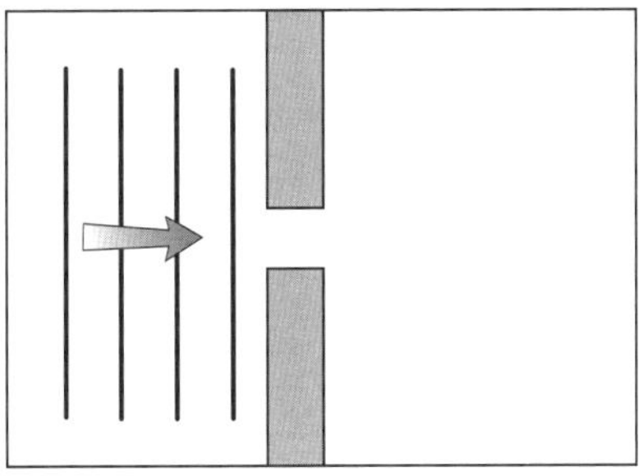

(2)

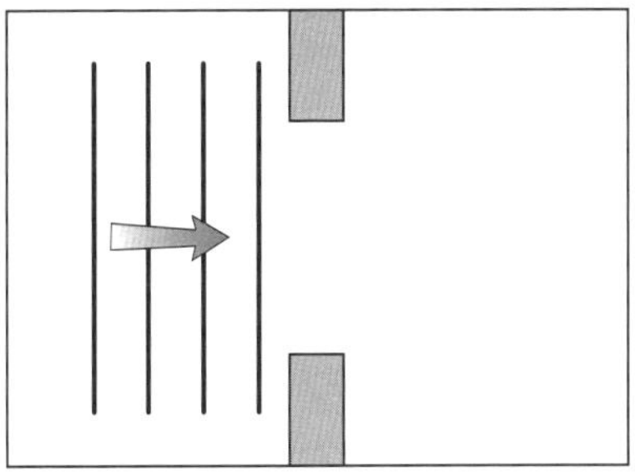

Top Tips: Wave questions often involve changes in **density**. You need to know how density changes affect wave **speed** — so you can work out if a wave refracts (and if so, which way) or is totally internally reflected. And don't forget that waves **diffract** too — but that's nothing to do with density.

Wave Interference

Q1 The diagrams below each show **displacement–time graphs** of two waves that are **overlapping**.

On each set of empty axes, draw what the graph of the combined wave would look like.
Also decide whether the interference is **constructive** or **destructive** — circle the correct answer.

a)

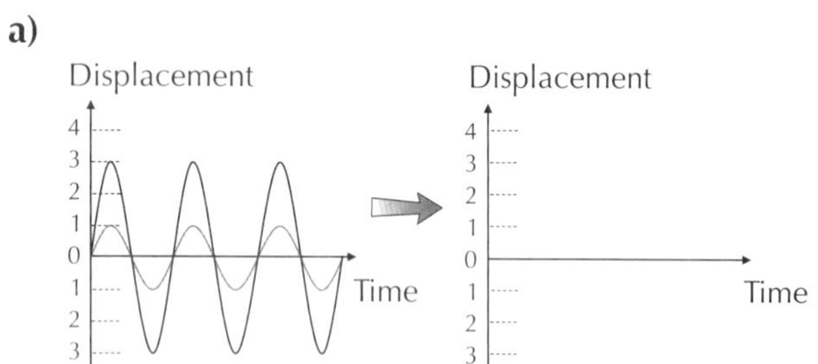

This is **constructive** / **destructive** interference.

b)

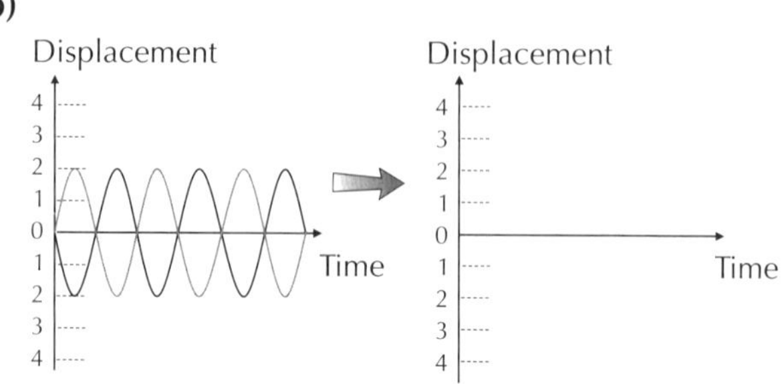

This is **constructive** / **destructive** interference.

Q2 Caleb was in a science lesson listening to a single musical note that his teacher was playing through a loudspeaker. To his surprise, when his teacher connected up **another speaker**, the sound got **quieter** rather than **louder**.

a) **Explain** what was happening to the two sound waves at the place where Caleb was sitting.

....

....

b) Caleb then got up and walked around the lab. Describe what he might have heard as he walked around.

....

....

Q3 **Laser light** was shone onto a screen through two very **thin slits** that were close together.

a) Describe what you would see on the screen.

....

b) The slits are much **closer together** than the loudspeakers in Q2. Why is this?

....

....

c) Which of these situations would give **destructive** interference? Circle the correct letter.

A A path difference of an odd number of whole wavelengths

B A path difference of an odd number of half wavelengths

C A path difference of an even number of half wavelengths.

Wave Interference

Q4 The diagram shows sets of overlapping waves produced by two dippers (d1 and d2) in a ripple tank. The **solid lines** indicate where there is a **peak** (or crest) and the **dashed lines** indicate where there is a **trough**.

a) For each point A-D decide whether there will be **constructive** or **destructive** interference. Underline the correct answer.

A constructive / destructive

B constructive / destructive

C constructive / destructive

D constructive / destructive

b) The wavelength of the waves is **1 cm**. A point, P, is 5 cm away from d1 and 8 cm away from d2.

Point P is not on the diagram, by the way.

i) What is the **path difference** at point P?

....

ii) How many **half wavelengths** fit into this path difference?

....

iii) Will there be **constructive** or **destructive** interference at point P?

....

c) The dippers were slowed down to produce a wavelength of 2 cm.

i) What is the **path difference** at point P now?

....

ii) How many **half wavelengths** fit into this path difference?

....

iii) Will there be **constructive** or **destructive** interference at point P?

....

Q5 Explain why the **interference** patterns produced by light show that it must act like a **wave**.

Think what would happen if light acted like particles and was beamed through two slits.

....

....

Top Tips: Wave interference is a bit of a crazy concept, but once you've got your head around it you can get lots of fairly straightforward marks in the exam.

Electromagnetic Radiation

Q1 Indicate whether the following statements are **true** or **false**.

		True	False
a)	Visible light travels faster in a vacuum than both X-rays and radio waves.	☐	☐
b)	The higher the frequency of a wave, the longer the wavelength.	☐	☐
c)	Radio waves have the shortest wavelength of all EM (electromagnetic) waves.	☐	☐

Q2 EM radiation occurs at many different wavelengths.

Complete the table to show the seven types of EM wave:

			VISIBLE LIGHT			
1m to 10^4 m	10^{-2} m	10^{-5} m	10^{-7} m	10^{-8} m	10^{-10} m	10^{-12} m

Q3 A beam of EM radiation can be thought of as being made up of waves or **photons**.

a) What are photons?

....

b) Complete the following sentence by filling in the missing words.

> The higher the .... of the radiation,
> the .... the amount of energy carried by the photons.

Q4 Trevor says, 'Why can't we **hear** the Sun when we can see the **light** it emits?'

Explain why it is not possible for sound waves from the Sun to travel through space.

....

....

Q5 The 'strength' of a beam of light is given by its **intensity**.

a) Which of the following is the correct definition of the intensity of a beam of EM radiation?

A The number of waves arriving every second.

B The number of photons arriving every second.

C The amount of energy delivered per second.

b) What **two things** does the intensity of a beam of radiation depend on?

....

Uses of EM Waves

Q1 **X-rays** are one type of EM radiation.

a) Complete the paragraph below, choosing from the words in the box.

bones	flesh	dense	more	less	shadow	light	ionising

Hospitals use X-rays to produce .... pictures to see if a patient has any broken bones. X-rays cannot pass easily through .... materials like .... and metal because they are absorbed by them. .... is .... dense, so it lets X-rays through more easily.

b) Write down one other use of X-rays.

....

Certificate of Birth
Ray

Q2 Information can be transmitted quickly through **optical fibres**.

a) Tick the boxes to show whether these statements are **true** or **false**.

	True	False
i) Optical fibres carry electromagnetic radiation.	☐	☐
ii) Optical fibres work because the light signal is refracted along the fibre.	☐	☐

b) Which of the following types of EM radiation are used in optical fibres?
Circle the correct answer(s).

Radio **Microwaves** **Visible Light** **Ultraviolet** **Infrared**

c) Apart from speed, give one advantage of using optical fibres to transmit a signal.

....

Q3 a) Explain why **radio waves** are good for transmitting data over large distances.

....

....

b) Write down one use of radio waves.

....

....

Uses of EM Waves

Q4 Sharon is heating up some **ready-made curry** in her **microwave** oven. Briefly explain how microwaves heat up the curry.

....

....

Q5 **Gabrielle** in London calls Carwyn in Toronto using her **satellite phone**.

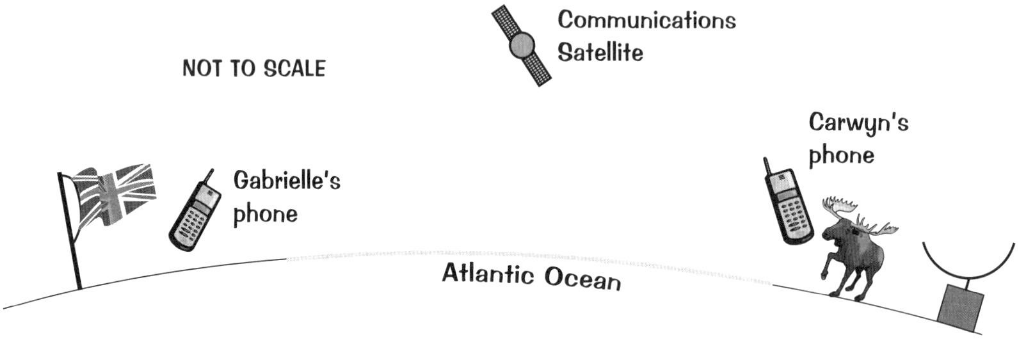

a) Number the following phrases 1 to 7 to explain how the signal reaches Carwyn's phone.

- [ ] The satellite absorbs the signal and then retransmits it to...
- [ ] ...Carwyn's phone.
- [ ] ...a communications satellite...
- [ ] ...near Toronto, which sends the signal to...
- [ ] ...a ground station...
- [ ] ...orbiting above the Earth's atmosphere.
- [1] Gabrielle's phone sends a microwave signal to...

b) Explain why ground-based satellite dishes are made of **metal**.

....

c) Why are **microwaves** used to transmit a signal to the satellite?

....

d) Give **one** reason why the same microwaves used to cook food cannot be used to transmit information between the transmitter and the satellite.

....

Top Tips: EM waves have a huge number of uses, but luckily you just need to know about six — radio, TV, satellite communications, microwave ovens, X-rays and optical fibres. It's not a short list, so make sure you know what type of wave is used where and, more specifically, why...

Adding Information to Waves

Q1 Complete the passage below using words from the list.

EM waves **visible light** **telephone lines** **infrared** **signals** **pressure waves**

For any information to be transmitted, it needs to be converted into .... Information can be carried along .... or broadcast through the air using .... It can also be carried using .... or .... waves transmitted through optical fibres.

Q2 Liz is listening to DJ Terry on Queenie FM.

a) What do the letters **FM** stand for?

....

b) Indicate whether the following statements about FM are **true** or **false**.

	True	False
i) An FM transmitter continually sends out a carrier wave.	☐	☐
ii) The signal changes the carrier wave by changing its amplitude.	☐	☐
iii) The signal is carried as changes in frequency of the combined wave.	☐	☐
iv) The transmitted signal will be picked up by a receiver.	☐	☐

c) What is the job of a **receiver**?

....

Q3 Long wavelength radio waves carry signals by **amplitude modulation**.

a) Explain what amplitude modulation means.

....

b) In the space below, sketch the shape of the **signal wave** and **carrier wave** that produced this shape.

Modulated carrier wave = Carrier wave + Signal wave

Analogue and Digital Signals

Q1 Fill in the blanks, choosing from the words below.

digital	analogue	amplified	weaken	interference	noise

All signals .... as they travel. To overcome this, they can be .... Signals may also suffer .... from other signals or from electrical disturbances. This causes .... in the signal. When signals are amplified, the noise is also amplified, but it's much harder to remove noise from a(n) .... signal.

Q2 Sketch: a 'clean' digital signal. a 'noisy' digital signal. a 'noisy' analogue signal.

Q3 a) Explain why it is better to send **digital** signals to a computer rather than analogue ones.

....

b) Explain why digital signals suffer less from **noise** than analogue signals.

....

....

c) State one other advantage of using digital signals for communication.

....

Q4 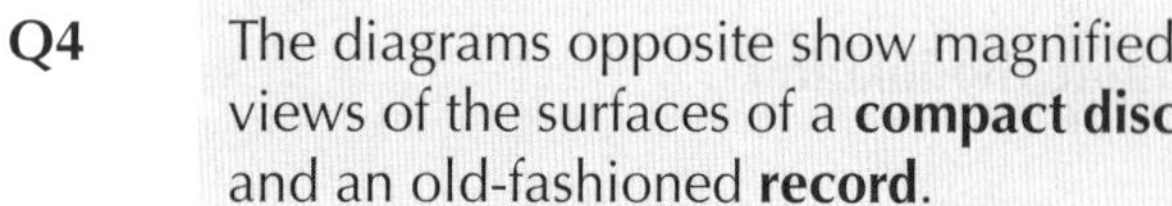
The diagrams opposite show magnified views of the surfaces of a **compact disc** and an old-fashioned **record**.

The CD is read by a laser, along the path shown by the arrow. The record is read by a needle which follows the grooves.

Both devices produce an electrical signal, which is then converted into sound.

For each device, sketch the type of trace you would expect to see on a monitor.

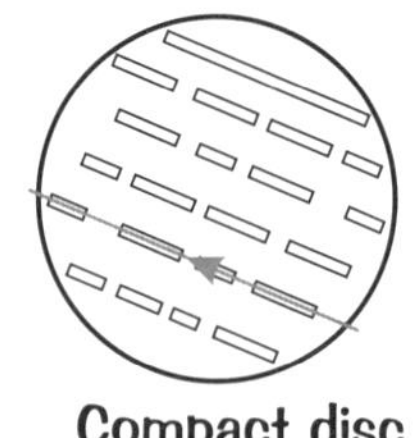
Compact disc

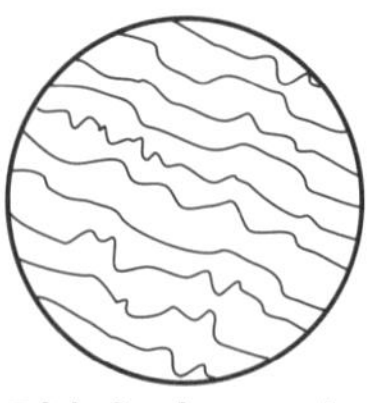
Old-fashioned record

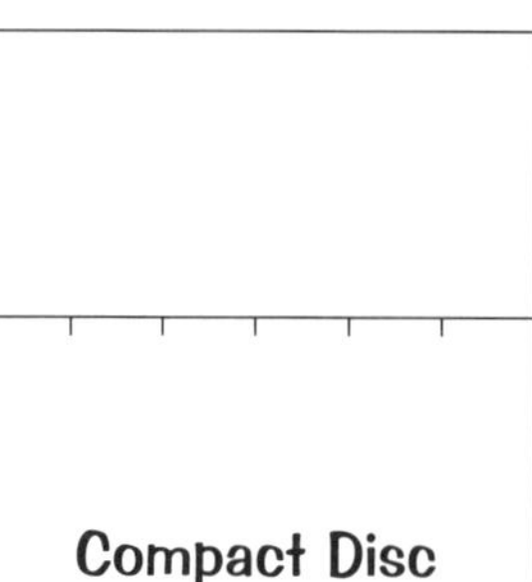

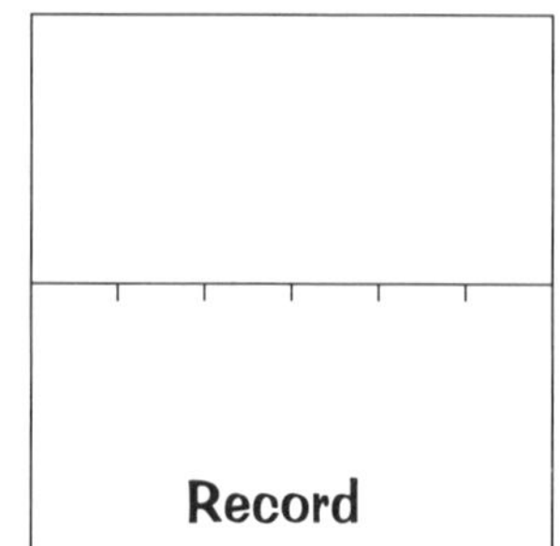

Broadband and Wireless Internet

Q1 Read the passage below and answer the questions that follow.

Broadband brings media to the masses

Broadband internet connections are becoming increasingly popular in rich countries such as the USA, Japan and the countries of Europe. Broadband allows more information to be sent and received per second than old-fashioned 'dial-up' internet connections, and is therefore much better suited to downloading media entertainment like music and movies.

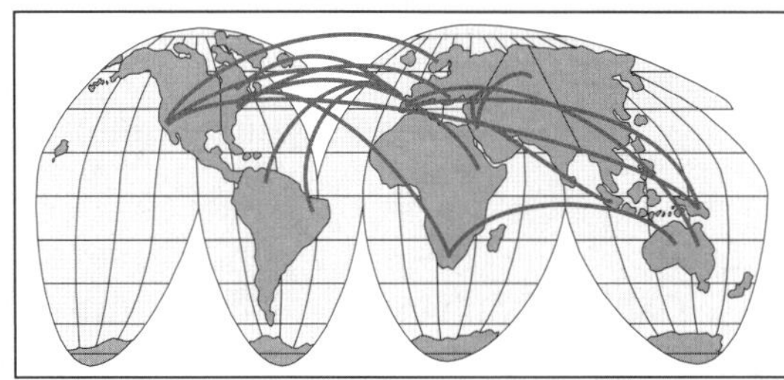

More than 14 million households in the UK have access to the internet (out of the country's 25 million or so households). Of these, approximately 75% have broadband.

There are two main types of broadband internet connection — DSL and cable. DSL involves information being sent along conventional (copper) phone lines, whereas cable connections use a combination of coaxial cable (a cable containing two conducting layers to reduce signal interference) and optical fibres.

Another popular piece of internet technology is known as a wireless router.

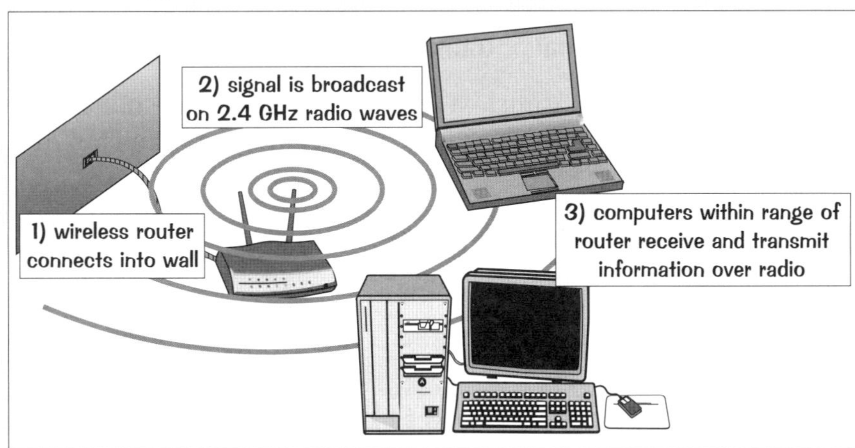

2) signal is broadcast on 2.4 GHz radio waves
1) wireless router connects into wall
3) computers within range of router receive and transmit information over radio

Wireless routers are plugged into a wall socket to gain access to the internet using the normal connection (whether it's via cable, DSL, or anything else). They then transmit the internet connection over a limited range (about 100 metres) using radio waves. Any computer within the range of the router can then communicate with it via radio, allowing users to get onto the internet without having their computer connected into a wall socket. The radio waves typically used by wireless routers have a frequency of about 2.4 GHz (2 400 000 000 Hz).

a) Using information from the article, suggest why broadband internet connections are becoming more popular.

....

....

Broadband and Wireless Internet

b) **i)** Using information from the article, estimate the **percentage** of UK households that have access to an internet connection.

....

ii) Approximately how many households in the UK have a **broadband** internet connection?

....

c) Cable broadband connections use **optical fibres** like the one shown below.

A

B

i) In the diagram above, which of the two labelled layers (A and B) is the **denser**? ....

ii) In which material, A or B, would light travel **faster**? ....

d) **Wireless routers** use radio waves to communicate with computers.

i) Are radio waves **longitudinal** or **transverse**? ....

ii) Using information from the article, calculate the wavelength of a typical wireless router's radio waves. (Speed of an EM wave ≈ 300 million m/s)

....

....

....

iii) What **type** of signal are the radio waves likely to carry? Explain your answer.

....

....

e) Wireless routers are sometimes used to provide internet access to an entire building, but they are also commonly used in individual households in tightly packed residential areas. Suggest why this might cause a **security** problem.

....

....

....